AA

ORDNANCE SURVEY
LEISURE GUIDE
CHANNEL ISLANDS

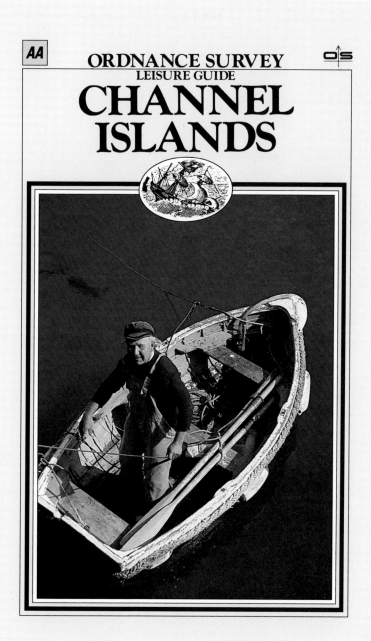

Produced jointly by the Publishing Division of the
Automobile Association and the Ordnance Survey

Cover: Les Minquiers, off Jersey (top);
Petit Bot, Guernsey (below left); Rozel, Jersey

Back cover: Fort Regent, Jersey

Title page: Fisherman, St Peter Port, Guernsey

Opposite: View from Castle Cornet, Guernsey

Introductory page: Farmhouse, St Peter's Valley, Jersey

Editor: Antonia Hebbert

Art Editor: Bob Johnson **Designer:** John Breeze

Editorial contributors: Alan Barber (Walks – Bailiwick of
Guernsey); Victor Coysh (The Story of the Channel Islands);
Tim Earl (Natural History; Gazetteer – Bailiwick of
Guernsey; short features); Sonia Hillsdon (Fortress Islands;
The German Occupation; The Seas around the Islands;
Islanders Today); Beth Lloyd (Gazetteer – Bailiwick of Jersey;
short features; Walks – Bailiwick of Jersey); La Société
Jersiaise/Marguerite Syvret (The Story of the Channel
Islands); Vicky Stuckey (Directory). Editorial consultants:
Richard Hocart, Richard Mayne

Picture researcher: Wyn Voysey

Original photography: Stuart Abraham, Peter Trenchard

Typeset by Avonset, Midsomer Norton, Bath.
Printed in Great Britain by Purnell Book Production
Limited. Member of the BPCC Group.

Maps extracted from the Ordnance Survey's Map of the
Channel Islands at 1:50 000 scale; Ordnance Survey/States of
Jersey Official Leisure Map of Jersey at 1:25 000 scale; D.Mil.
Survey mapping of Guernsey at 1:25 000 scale; D.Mil. Survey
mapping of Alderney, Sark, Herm and Jethou at
1:10 000/10 560 scale. Reproduced with the kind permission
of Her Majesty's Stationery Office. Crown Copyright reserved.

Additions to the maps by the Cartographic Dept of the
Automobile Association and the Ordnance Survey.

Produced by the Publishing Division of the Automobile
Association.

Distributed in the United Kingdom by the Ordnance Survey,
Southampton, and the Publishing Division of the
Automobile Association, Fanum House, Basingstoke,
Hampshire RG21 2EA.

The contents of this publication are believed correct at the
time of printing. Nevertheless, the Publishers cannot accept
responsibility for errors or omissions, or for changes in
details given.

AA ISBN 0 86145 515 0 (hardback)
AA ISBN 0 86145 514 2 (softback)
OS ISBN 0 319 00124 5 (hardback)
OS ISBN 0 319 00123 7 (softback)

Published by the Automobile Association and the
Ordnance Survey.

AA ref: 53992 (hardback)
AA ref: 53989 (softback)

CHANNEL ISLANDS

Contents

Using this Book

The entries in the Gazetteer have been carefully
selected to reflect the interest and variety of the
Channel Islands. The five main islands are
arranged in order of size. Jersey and Guernsey are
divided into threee sections each, within which
places of interest are given in alphabetical order.
Both French and English spellings are used.

Each entry in the A to Z Gazetteer has the atlas
page number on which the place can be found and
its grid reference. An explanation of how to use
the grid is given on page 82.

Beneath many of the entries in the Gazetteer are
listed AA-recommended hotels, restaurants,
garages, camping sites and guesthouses in the
immediate vicinity of the place described.
Hotels, restaurants and camping sites are also given
an AA classification.

HOTELS
1-star   Good hotels and inns, generally of
small scale and with acceptable
facilities and furnishing.

2-star   Hotels offering a higher standard of
accommodation, with some private
bathrooms/shower; lavatories on all
floors; wider choice of food.

3-star   Well-appointed hotels; a good
proportion of bedrooms with private
bathrooms/showers.

4-star   Exceptionally well-appointed hotels
offering a high standard of comfort
and service, the majority of bedrooms
should have private
bathrooms/showers.

5-star   Luxury hotels offering the highest
international standards.

Hotels often satisfy *some* of the requirements for
higher classifications than that awarded.

Red-star   Red stars denote hotels which are
considered to be of outstanding merit
within their classification.

Country   A hotel where a relaxed informal
House   atmosphere prevails. Some of the
Hotel   facilities may differ from those at
urban hotels of the same classification.

RESTAURANTS
1-fork   Modest but good restaurant.
2-fork   Restaurant offering a higher standard
of comfort than above.
3-fork   Well-appointed restaurant.
4-fork   Exceptionally well-appointed
restaurant.
5-fork   Luxury restaurant.
1-rosette   Hotel or restaurant where the cuisine
is considered to be of a higher
standard than is expected in an
establishment within its classification.

2-rosette   Hotel or restaurant offering very much
above average food irrespective of the
classification.
3-rosette   Hotel or restaurant offering
outstanding food, irrespective of
classification.

GUESTHOUSES
These are different from, but not necessarily
inferior to, AA-appointed hotels, and they offer an
alternative for those who prefer inexpensive and
not too elaborate accommodation. They all
provide clean, comfortable accommodation in
homely surroundings. Each establishment must
usually offer at least six bedrooms and there
should be a general bathroom and a general toilet
for every six bedrooms without private facilities.

Parking facilities should be reasonably close.

Other requirements include:
Well maintained exterior, clean and hygienic
kitchens; good standard of furnishing; friendly and
courteous service; access at reasonable times; the
use of a telephone and full English breakfast.

CAMPING SITES
1-pennant Site licence; 10% of pitches for
touring units; site density not more
than 30 per acre; 2 separate toilets for
each sex per 30 pitches; good quality
tapwater; efficient waste disposal;
regular cleaning of ablutions block; fire
precautions; well-drained ground.
2-pennant All one-pennant facilities plus: 2
washbasins with hot and cold water
for each sex per 30 pitches in separate
washrooms; warden available at certain
times of the day.
3-pennant All two-pennant facilities plus: one
shower or bath for each sex per 30
pitches, with hot and cold water;
electric shaver points and mirrors; all-
night lighting of toilet blocks; deep
sinks for washing clothes; facilities for
buying milk, bread and gas; warden in
attendance by day, on call by night.
4-pennant All three-pennant facilities plus: a
higher degree of organisation than
one–three-pennant sites; attention to
landscaping; reception office; late-
arrivals enclosure; first aid hut; shop;
routes to essential facilities lit after
dark; play area; bad weather shelter;
hard standing for touring vans.
5-pennant A comprehensive range of services and
equipment; careful landscaping;
automatic laundry; public telephone;
indoor play facilities for children; extra
facilities for recreation; warden in
attendance 24 hours per day.

CHANNEL ISLANDS

Introduction

'Pieces of France which fell into the sea and were picked up by England . . .' wrote Victor Hugo of the Channel Islands, and today they still have a unique atmosphere that continues to charm both visitors and Islanders themselves.

This guide introduces the rich heritage and traditions of the Channel Islands, with information on wildlife, what to do, places to visit, maps, walks and drives.

Written entirely by people who live and work in the Channel Islands, backed by the AA's research and by up-to-date mapping, this guide should be equally useful to first-time visitors, Channel Islanders and those who are drawn back here year after year.

The Story of the Channel Islands

A hundred miles south of England and tucked into the elbow of France lie the Channel Islands: Jersey, Guernsey, Alderney, Sark, Herm and Jethou, as well as numerous islets. They have become famous for their tourist attractions, the role they played in World War II and, not least, their importance in the realms of finance. These favoured isles have always held an attraction to others, whether it be people of the Stone Age, French invaders, conquering Germans or today's settlers and banking barons. Despite or perhaps because of their eventful past, in the late 20th century the islands enjoy elements of independence, prosperity and a sense of contentment.

In the archaeological history of western Europe, La Cotte de Saint Brelade in Jersey is a site of major importance. Here a raised beach a quarter of a million years old illustrates the fluctuating sea levels of the Pleistocene period when the island intermittently formed part of the Continent. Discoveries at La Cotte include the bones of mammoth and woolly rhinoceros, evidence of plant life in the last inter-glacial period and artefacts and teeth of Neanderthal man.

Over 6000 years ago, Neolithic people made the Channel Islands their home. They were farmers, and while no trace of their homes survives, ample evidence of their burial places are to be seen. The most ancient is at Les Fouaillages, on Guernsey's L'Ancresse Common. It was discovered in 1976 and it may date from as early as 4500BC. Nearby are other megaliths, notably the passage grave of La Varde, another at Le Déhus, a mile away, and Creux ès Faies.

The standing stones of the Channel Islands include two stone figures carved in the shape of women, which may well have been prehistoric idols, in the churchyards of Guernsey's St Martin and Castel. Jersey has a group of standing stones at Les Quennevais and Les Blanches Banques. There was a time when these monumental standing stones or 'menhirs' were even more plentiful in the Channel Islands than they are today, but many have been broken up for building stone in more recent times.

Jersey is also rich in Neolithic graves, the most important being at La Hougue Bie where, beneath

Mont Orgueil Castle commands this eastern Jersey coastline

two medieval chapels on an artificial mound, excavations in 1924 revealed an important passage grave. Other notable sites are the dolmens of Le Couperon, Faldouet, Le Mont Ubé, Les Monts, Grantez, and La Sergenté, St Brelade.

Alderney must have been a favourite burial place for early people, for records reveal that there were numerous graves there. Unhappily they have almost all disappeared, many being destroyed in the last century during the island's re-fortification. The sole monument of note is a cist, 'La Roc à l'Epine', the survivor of a group which stood on the site of the present Fort Tourgis. Little remains of the dolmens of Les Pourciaux, at Longis, but nearby, at Les Huguettes, early Iron Age pottery was found in 1968.

Two megaliths may survive on Sark, although some archaeologists are sceptical and declare that these may be natural rock formations. Yet in Little Sark, above Clouet Bay, it seems obvious that a ruined cist stands on the cliffside. A great capstone rests on lesser boulders, more convincing than its fellow monument, at La Vermandaye, close by.

Herm's northern region, by contrast, is rich in megalithic tombs, and six stand on the Common and on adjoining hill tops. Some think that Herm, like larger Alderney, had some religious significance in prehistoric times and that to be buried there was a privilege for those living in present-day France. But modern archaeological thought is that Herm's tombs were built by and for its inhabitants.

From later centuries, a cache of bronze weapons was unearthed in 1976 in St Lawrence, Jersey, and a magnificent gold torque was discovered in St Helier in 1889.

Numerous coins dug up on island sites and a Gallo-Roman building at the foot of the Pinnacle Rock in north-west Jersey give evidence of a Roman presence in Jersey, which, under Augustus, formed part of Lugdunensis and was governed from distant Lyons. The Channel Islands were familiar to Roman voyagers hugging the coast of the northerly outposts but for long it was assumed that if the Romans ever inhabited the Channel Islands it was only in Alderney. At the ancient fort known as the Nunnery (something it never was) a wall reveals herringbone masonry, suggesting that here could have been a Roman station, rather than a settlement. Some archaeologists thought that Alderney had other sites indicating Roman occupation and traces of their artefacts have been found there. Significant Roman remains were discovered only quite recently. In 1984, at St Peter Port, stonework was unearthed near the shore, which archaeologists pronounced to be of Roman origin. Coins, pottery and other discoveries appear to confirm this belief and in the same year the remains of a Roman galley were found on the seabed just outside St Peter Port. The site in the town was probably a substantial Roman settlement.

Saints and Norsemen
The period between the Roman occupation and the arrival of the Normans is somewhat obscure, since substantial traces of life at that time are scarce and written records are non-existent. Tradition asserts that in about 555 St Sampson, Bishop of Dol, in Normandy, brought Christianity to Guernsey, landing on the shore beside the site of the church dedicated to him. His cousin, St Magloire, is believed to have established a monastery in Sark at about that time.

Left: the St Helier gold torque before restoration – now in the Jersey Museum
Below: La Hougue Bie – a 50ft-long passage grave built about 3000BC

To the first missionaries Jersey was known as Angia. Traditionally Saint Helier brought Christianity to Jersey about the same time as St Sampson did to Guernsey. He lived on the Hermitage rock behind Elizabeth Castle and was martyred by Saxon pirates. Celtic missionaries from Britain also came to Jersey, among them Branwalader, who gave his name to the church and parish of Saint Brelade, and Saint Magloire, traditionally known locally as St Mannelier, who gave his name to the ancient grammar school of Saint Mannelier. Its endowments, when it ceased to exist, were vested in scholarships to the much younger Victoria College.

Little else is known about the Channel Islands in the Dark Ages, but the ancient parish boundaries predate the arrival of the Normans, the outline of whose fiefs form a different tracery on the map of the islands.

The Norman heritage

The islands were subject to Viking raids in the 9th century and some of their place-names have a Norse origin. Their word for island was 'ey', the ending of 'Guernsey', 'Jersey' and 'Alderney', while 'hou' (Jethou, Burhou, Lihou) suggested smaller islands.

When Charles the Simple ceded Normandy to Rollo the Channel Islands were not included, but in 933 Rollo's son, William Longsword, annexed from the Bretons the Cotentin peninsula and the islands to the west. For a century and a half they formed part of the Duchy of Normandy. Indeed, to this day if islanders believe there is wrongful interference with their property, they may raise the ancient *clameur de haro*, invoking the aid of the 'prince'. This acts as a restraining order on the alleged wrongdoer, until the case can be brought to court.

None before or since have left so great a mark on the community as have the Normans. They gave the islands their ancient language of Norman-French, their customary laws and love of litigation, a seafaring tradition, and distinctive surnames which survive to this day.

Well before 1066 Norman abbeys held property in the islands, and there is proof that they had parish churches by 1042. They were first in the See of Dol and later that of Coutances.

When Duke William conquered England in 1066 he continued to be Normandy's ruler and Islanders tended to regard him as their duke although official documents referred to 'their lord the King'. The Conquest, at first, must have made little difference to their way of life which was as much Norman as that existing across the water, and until less than a century ago the use of Norman-French among Islanders was common. It is still spoken by some older Islanders and is not like modern French: preserved in the isolation of the islands, it is closer to the language of Duke William and his followers. The island tongue differed in some degree between one island and another, but today, unfortunately, it is fast dying out.

Feudalism

The Norman dukes introduced this form of local government and land tenure into the Channel Islands before 1066. The duke, owner of the archipelago, apportioned areas, known as 'fiefs' to certain important persons who, in return, paid dues in personal service or in kind. For their part, they sublet parts of their domains to 'tenants', who paid the 'seigneurs' (lords of the manor) also in kind, tilling the land, paying dues for use of the seigneurial mill, yet enjoying anything but a serf-like existence. The system worked well, for it meant that the islands were self-supporting. St Ouen's Manor in Jersey is still owned by a lineal descendant of the first de Carteret to hold land as a seigneur from the king. The seigneurs continued to enjoy their ancient privileges, until in the 20th century the last of the seigneurial rights were abolished. Their special relationship to the sovereign is recognised at the sitting of Jersey's Assize d'Héritage, the oldest land court in Europe.

In some measure, the island seigneurs were responsible for local defence. While this 'citizen army' was primarily for insular protection, it could be summoned overseas were the duke taken captive. To a certain extent, the feudal system meant self-government, since feudal courts were held at certain times, at which tenants played important roles. In Guernsey the master body was the Court of Chief Pleas, when seigneurs paid suit of service to the duke, although he was not present in person.

The Church played an important role in island life, since Norman abbeys controlled its religious aspect and some of them were seigneurs of important fiefs and did very well out of their revenues. Until the Tudor period tithes were paid, except in time of war, to the Norman abbeys and to the Bishop of Coutances whose diocese included the islands. The rolls of the Norman Exchequer for 1180 reveal how taxes were collected.

After Normandy

History changed dramatically when, in 1204, King John lost mainland Normandy and the Channel Islands became an outpost of great strategic importance. Distance from England reduced the visitations of itinerant justices who had hitherto travelled from nearby Normandy, and the islands acquired a measure of self-government independent of the seigneurial courts, which continued to function. Two Bailiwicks were established (Guernsey's included Alderney and Sark) under a warden, captain or governor who in time delegated part of his duties to a bailiff. Twelve jurats, elected from prominent Islanders, supported the bailiff in administering the law. From this embryo court have evolved the States and Royal Courts as they function today.

Jersey's parochial system has its origins in this period. It is based on a hierarchy of unpaid officers rising from constable's officer to vingtenier, centenier and finally constable, who is the civil head of the parish.

Now that France had become a potential enemy, defences on a large scale were begun. Guernsey's major stronghold was Castle Cornet, Jersey's Mont Orgueil. Early in the Middle Ages the French attempted to regain the islands and savage raids were made on them. Usually they failed in their objective, but between 1340 and 1345 the French occupied Guernsey. Probably as a result, Edward III ordered that St Peter Port be a walled town. No traces of a wall survive.

In 1373 Bertrand du Guesclin, Constable of France, invaded and held Jersey to ransom. In 1461, during the Wars of the Roses, Mont Orgueil was captured by Jean Carbonnel whose cousin the Comte de Maulévrier was plotting with Henry VI's queen, Marguerite of Anjou, in support of the

Sir Anthony Poulett, Governor of Jersey from 1590 to 1600

Lancastrians. This time the French held Jersey for seven years. So much did the islands suffer at the hands of pirates and adventurers that in 1481 Pope Sixtus IV declared them neutral in a papal bull. After that they were to prove a convenient source of clandestine communication between England and France. In recognition of the islands' steadfast loyalty to the English Crown, successive kings and queens renewed the charters which confirmed the ancient rights and privileges enjoyed by Islanders 'from time immemorial'.

Medieval Alderney was poorly defended and fell an easy prey to marauders. The building of Essex Castle did little to mend matters. Sark was often invaded and occupied by the French, and there were times when it was almost uninhabited. Its defences were virtually nil and pirates made it their haunt.

The Tudors
Protestantism reached the islands under Edward VI, but in Guernsey during the reign of Queen Mary there was a shocking example of intolerance when, in 1556, a woman and her two daughters were burnt at the stake on a trumped-up charge of heresy. One of them gave birth in her agony and even the new-born babe was consigned to the flames. This was also the plight of 'witches' and torture was freely practised on their being found guilty by the Royal Court.

In the reign of Elizabeth I Huguenot refugees brought Calvinism to the islands, and set up a regime which profoundly influenced the civil and ecclesiastical administration. Although England attempted to force Islanders to adopt its system of worship, a special form of Presbyterianism was practised for many years by French Protestant pastors, who were understood by the non-English-speaking Islanders.

A new outlook
In the reign of Elizabeth I, the pirates' haunt of Sark was colonised by Jerseyman Helier de Carteret. In 1565 his offer to do so was welcomed by the sovereign, who granted him a charter and made him seigneur. Forty 'tenants' helped to re-colonise the island, and as well as making Sark fertile, they also defended it. For this transformation the island was given a form of

home rule which still exists.

Before this time the Channel Islands had been self-supporting, with little contact with the outside world; inter-marriage was common, for roads were bad and communication with neighbouring islands was not easy.

During the Elizabethan period, things began to change. Elizabethan Jerseymen developed a prosperous trade with the New World. Merchants also had links with Southampton where traffic in wool gave so great a boost to the knitting and export of stockings that laws were passed in Jersey to ensure that essential work on the land was not neglected.

In 1563, Elizabeth I founded the college of her name in Guernsey. Elsewhere, schools helped to broaden the Islanders' outlook and the development of harbours promoted a measure of commerce and resultant prosperity.

Civil War
It might be supposed that the English Civil War would have had little impact on Islanders, but this was not so. While Alderney and Sark were scarcely involved, Guernsey and Jersey certainly were.

Guernsey favoured the Parliamentarian side of the struggle, but the Royalist Governor, Sir Peter Osborne, refused to submit and defended Castle Cornet against the rest of Guernsey. From 1643 to 1651 a state of siege prevailed and at times there were exchanges of fire between castle and town. In 1651 its gallant garrison surrendered with all the honours of war.

From Jersey we have a vivid contemporary picture of the conflict from the diary of Jean Chevalier. Through the intervention of Sir Walter Raleigh, sometime Governor of Jersey, Mont Orgueil had been reprieved from proposed demolition when Elizabeth Castle was built as the main centre of defence. From there Sir George Carteret held out for the Royalists, twice giving refuge to the two sons of Charles I. Immediately after the king's execution, a document which still exists was read by the vicomte, Laurens Hamptonne, to proclaim Charles II king in Jersey. Although Sir George had finally to yield to the Parliamentarian Admiral Blake, he was rewarded at the Restoration by a gift of land in America which he named New Jersey. Also at the Restoration Charles II gave Jersey the Royal Mace (still used today) in acknowledgment of its loyalty, while Guernsey, despite its opposition to the Crown, had its ancient rights and privileges restored.

Alderney had been held by Parliamentary troops during the Civil War when it was governed by members of the Chamberlain family. The king subsequently granted the island to three Jersey Royalists, who later transferred their rights to Sir George Carteret. It was at this period that Alderney ceased to be governed by Guernsey, and not until 1825 did it stop having its own Governor.

Riches from the sea
Trade with France was forbidden under William III (who thereby overrode the 15th-century papal declaration of neutrality) and this gave impetus to the contraband business. It was a profitable source of island revenue, with high English duties on wines, spirits and tobacco giving mariners from the islands an incentive to 'run' contraband across the Channel. Their efforts were made easy in one direction, since a blind eye was turned on them by

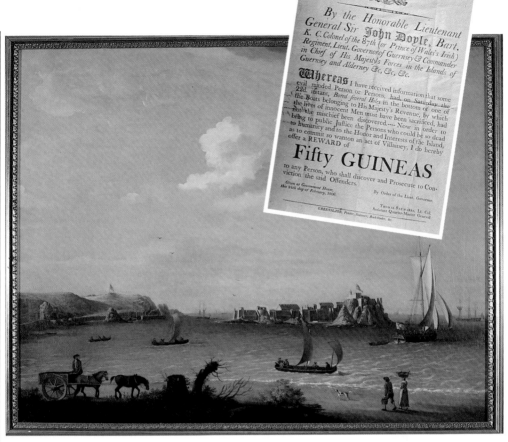

Elizabeth Castle – from the painting 'La Mont de la Ville' by Dominique Serres, now in the Jersey Museum. Inset: an 1806 reward notice from Guernsey

insular authorities. It was not an offence to import such goods into the islands, and what happened to them afterwards was not their business.

By then, however, local merchants were sailing further afield. When the British won Canada from the French, island fishing enterprises were set up on the Gaspé coast and in Newfoundland. During the wars with France, Islanders made fortunes when they were granted 'Letters of Marque', authorising masters of their vessels to attack and seize enemy ships and to share in the resultant spoils. One such privateer, owned by Alderney Governor John Le Mesurier, brought in prizes worth nearly £135,000 and this fortune enabled important improvements to be made to Alderney's Braye harbour. Jersey and Guernsey privateers were equally fortunate, and the resultant prosperity can be seen in the fine houses built at that period.

While the traders grew rich, the poor often suffered hardship. There were two major revolts in Jersey: one in 1730 against the devaluation of the *sou* (Jersey's currency was based on the French *livre tournois* until 1834), and one in 1769 against a rise in the price of bread. A petition to the King in Council resulted in the Code of 1771, which was designed to be a full statement of the laws then in force, and defined the roles of Court and States, separating to some extent the legislative and executive functions of government.

John Wesley

Methodism gained a strong hold in the major islands towards the close of the 18th century and it was strengthened by the visit of John Wesley to Alderney, Guernsey and Jersey. Chapels were built and French-speaking pastors, mainly Island men, were involved in the spread of nonconformism. In Sark, influenced by an earlier Huguenot pastor, Methodism was also strong.

The threat from France

Meanwhile the constant threat from France led to massive fortification schemes and to the arrival of English troops to reinforce the militias, newly reformed but dating back to Edward III. In Jersey a French invasion force under Baron de Rullecourt landed in January 1781 and was defeated in the Royal Square by the young Major Francis Peirson and the Jersey Militia – the still vividly remembered 'Battle of Jersey'.

During the French Revolution Admiral d'Auvergne, a Jerseyman, organised the rescue of French noble families and ran a secret service between the Royalists and the British Government which provided funds and arms to assist the Chouan uprising in Brittany. Fort Regent, military roads and larger harbours were built in the Napoleonic Wars.

In Guernsey, Fort George was built and numerous other forts, towers, batteries, signal stations and barracks were constructed. Coastal forces were manned by the militia and a strong garrison was also stationed in the major islands. A naval squadron was established off St Peter Port.

Guernsey's Governor, Sir John Doyle, was responsible for the improvement of the roads for easier troop and artillery movements. He was also instrumental in reclaiming the Braye du Valle, the channel which cut off Guernsey's northern part and made it a likely landing place for the French.

The peaceful years

After Napoleon's defeat at Waterloo, the island scene changed markedly. Gone were most of the troops and a new way of life began with the introduction of steam vessels, and with them tourists and English settlers. The steamers also carried perishable cargoes to England and thus

On 1 October 1969 the States of Guernsey Post Office Board became responsible for postal services in the Bailiwick. Attractive definitive sets are issued four times a year and are very popular with collectors

fostered the islands' horticultural industry.

Alderney underwent a massive (and unnecessary) re-fortification against the French in the 1840s due to the French extending Cherbourg as a naval harbour, but largely these were years of peace and expansion of trade and industry. It was hoped that fortunes would be made when silver was discovered in Little Sark in 1836. Mining continued feverishly for some years and the venture was financially supported by Seigneur Ernest Le Pelley. But when the mines failed in 1847 he was forced to sell the Seigneurie to the Collings family, whose most notable member was Dame Sibyl Hathaway.

The fishing trade reached its peak in the 1860s and provided employment for younger sons who emigrated to work for island firms in Canada, as well as local shipbuilders and clerks. Attracted by the climate and lack of taxation, English residents settled in the islands; French labour was recruited to help on the farms and Irish workers for the

building trade as the towns of St Peter Port and St Helier grew larger.

The islands adapted to change. When steam replaced sail, when the cod and the more local oyster trade languished, the development of the 'Guernsey Tom' and Jersey Royal potato, and the successful breeding of cattle for export boosted agriculture. In Jersey over the centuries open fields had been enclosed and cider orchards had made way for early potatoes and outdoor tomatoes but local laws of inheritance kept the manors and farms intact, with a sprinkling of more sophisticated Regency houses to proclaim increasing wealth. For the most part, the face of Guernsey had become one of many smallholdings. In the late 19th century the 'growing industry' grew rapidly. Traditional farming continued (at that time the export of cattle was important), but the cultivation of first grapes, and later tomatoes, was of much greater significance. Many an Islander became a part-time grower and often a dairy farmer was a grower also.

At the turn of the century, the country scene was still one in which farmers' wives in black sunbonnets milked in the fields, and neighbours joined forces in the early spring when as many as

*A photograph from the past – coal ships in
St Peter Port*

14 horses might pull the plough. World War I,
which cost the islands dear, heralded an
acceleration of the rate of change: the horse gave
way to the motor, buses ousted the 19th-century
railways and tramways, air traffic required airports.
Yet peaceful conditions and an enjoyable prosperity
seemed all set to last indefinitely, until in 1939 war
clouds darkened the horizon and the islands' well-
being was in jeopardy. At first all seemed to be
quiet and it was even suggested that people might
still visit the islands as before to escape the effects
of the war to some extent.

How futile such hopes were was proved in the
summer of 1940, when the latest great chapter in
Channel Islands' history opened. It was their
occupation by the forces of Germany.

Island government today

The forms of government in the Channel Islands
differ markedly. There is some resemblance
between those of Guernsey and Jersey, but the
constitutions of Alderney and Sark are quite
dissimilar. Despite the ancient origin of the system,
the administration of the Channel Islands keeps
abreast of the times and their unquestioned
prosperity must be the envy of the world.

The islands manage their internal affairs, subject,
not to Parliament, but to the King or Queen in
Council. The words of the historian Falle, writing
about Jersey, can be applied to all the islands: they
remain 'a Peculiar of the Crown' but they are not,
nor ever were, a 'parcel of the Realm of England'.

The Channel Islands are divided into two
Bailiwicks, those of Jersey and Guernsey, each with
a Lieutenant-Governor. The Bailiwick of Guernsey
includes Alderney and Sark. The Lieutenant-
Governor is the Queen's representative – the link
between the island and the Home Office – and has
a seat but no voice nor vote in States' Meetings.
Each Bailiwick has a Bailiff who presides at States

A view from the quay, St Helier, 1832

assemblies (the equivalent of parliament), and has
a Deputy.

Also present are the Crown Officers: in
Guernsey they are HM Procureur, HM
Comptroller, HM Greffier and Sheriff; in Jersey
they are known as Attorney General and Solicitor
General. They, with the Dean have a voice but no
vote. Also present at the Guernsey States are
Conseillers, Deputies and douzaine representatives
(a douzaine is a parish council) and two
representatives of the States of Alderney, because
Guernsey has some responsibility for its finances.
The Jersey States, reconstituted in 1948, are
attended by Senators, Constables and Deputies.

The States of Alderney have a President (holding
office for three years) and 12 members, elected
triennially. A Clerk and Treasurer also attend its
monthly meetings.

Sark still has a feudal system; it owes its
allegiance to the Queen through the Governor of
Guernsey. The Seigneur appoints the Seneschal,
who is President of Chief Pleas. The Seigneur also
attends the meetings, normally held three times a
year. The Seneschal is supported by the Prévôt
(sheriff) and Greffier and there are also 40 'tenants'
(property owners) and 12 Deputies, elected
triennially.

Fortifications: see page 14.
German Occupation: see page 16.

Fortress Islands

Today the chief invaders of the Channel Islands are its holidaymakers, who come back year after year hoping to bask on the beaches and sun-baked rocks or seek out the seabirds and wild flowers of the cliffs. Yet even the most dedicated holidaymaker must be aware of the islands' turbulent past. Strung right round the beautiful coastlines of Jersey, Guernsey and Alderney (and curiously adding interest rather than detracting from the scene) are fortifications of all ages, from medieval and Tudor castles to Napoleonic 'Martello' towers and gun emplacements only a few decades old.

When they belonged to the Duchy of Normandy, the fertile islands in the bay of Mont St Michael seemed to medieval pirates to lie there just for the picking. To begin with, especially in the summer months, the chief raiders were the Vikings. Throughout the 9th century they came in their longboats to ravage the coast of both France and England – taking in the Channel Isles en route.

Castles on the coast

In later years, after King John had lost the Duchy of Normandy, and the Channel Islanders had elected to stay under English rule, the enemy was France. Between 1204 and the mid-1400s the French not only launched a series of hit-and-run raids but also mounted several invasions against their former territories. From time to time they even succeeded in recapturing them.

For the stricken Channel Islanders, the answer was to fortify those eastern areas facing France which seemed most vulnerable. King John ordered the Governor of the Channel Islands, Hasculf de Suligny, to build two castles and as a result the approach to St Peter Port in Guernsey came to be guarded by Castle Cornet and the east coast of Jersey by Gorey (Gouray) Castle (Mont Orgeuil). Both were besieged from time to time, even captured, but for the most part they gave the Islanders the protection they needed.

Henry VIII saw the Channel Islands as a first line of defence against his Continental enemies, and appointed a commission to look into the military security of the islands. It advised not only a new fort in St Aubin's Bay (Jersey) to protect the large amount of shipping there, but also the erection of towers in the castles of Cornet and Mont Orgeuil, whose Tudor outline can still be distinguished today. In Alderney, Essex Castle was begun, to which each new generation of defenders added its own improvements.

It was Henry VIII's daughter Elizabeth I who agreed, on the advice of the great military engineer Paul Ivy, to the last of the great Tudor fortifications of the Channel Islands. Even in her father's time, Jersey's Mont Orgeuil was no longer proof against the newly invented cannon; nor did it in anyway safeguard on the south coast the rapidly growing town of St Helier. Plans had been passed in 1550 to protect the town by making a bulwark of the islet on which the decaying priory of St Helier stood. But no building had been done. The Queen contributed £500 to the scheme and when Jersey's governor, Sir Walter Raleigh, finally took up residence in the new fortification, he wrote to her that he had christened it 'The Castle Fort Isabella Bellissima' in her honour. It soon became known, and still is today, as Elizabeth Castle.

The Napoleonic threat

The next period of concentrated defence building began in 1778, when France declared itself an ally of the American colonists in their fight for independence, and thereby declared war on Britain.

Jersey's tower building began in 1778, when the Governor, General Conway, put forward a plan for 30 towers around the coast. Survivors include Seymour Tower, just over a mile off La Rocque and unusual in being square. The other 18th-century towers, such as the ones at First Tower and L'Archirondel, were built to a design which may have been General Conway's: about 35ft in diameter at the base and tapering at the top to about 29ft. They usually housed one 18-pound cannon and would have been serviced by an officer and 10 men, also accommodated in the tower.

The accelerated building of military installations in Jersey gained further importance from an actual

High on its hill, Castle Cornet offers some of the best views over Guernsey

Right: the First Tower, Jersey, one of 30 towers built around the coastline from 1779 to 1835
Far right: Kempt Tower and information centre, on the west coast of Jersey
Below: Fort Ile de Raz, now converted to flats, to the south of Longy Common, Alderney
Below right: cannons guarding Elizabeth Castle

French invasion. In 1781, a raiding party led by the adventurer de Rullecourt not only landed at La Rocque but got as far as St Helier without the alarm being raised. The island might have been lost, but for the bravery of young Major Peirson who led the defending forces and died, with de Rullecourt, in the struggle.

The dozens of coastal towers built in the next four decades are commonly referred to as 'Martello' towers. The true Martello tower is a squat round tower with few gun slits. More common in the islands are the taller round towers with gun slits in two storeys. These are also known as 'Martello' towers by the Islanders and they date from the American War of Independence.

Examples of true Martello towers, built specifically against the threat of invasion by Napoleon, include Kempt Tower in Jersey and Fort Grey in Guernsey. The other seven built in

Jersey include the Martello towers at Ouaisne, Noir Mont and La Grande Collette. Other genuine Martello towers in Guernsey are at Fort Houmet and Fort Saumarez. Fort Regent in Jersey, Fort Le Marchant in Guernsey and Fort Doyle in Alderney also date from this time.

The Telegraph Tower was built in Alderney for wartime communication with Guernsey and Jersey via Sark. By the end of the Napoleonic wars Alderney, with a population of just over 1000, was preparing for defence. Even with Napoleon's defeat, fears of invasion were not allayed for long. Twenty-five years later, the French built a strong naval base at Cherbourg. The British government's answer was to turn Alderney into 'the Gibraltar of the Channel Isles', by pouring millions of pounds into the small island. Among the defences built were Forts Albert and Clonque, a breakwater and a harbour at Braye, deep enough for the new ironclad warships. The demand for a labour force to build the fortifications and for a garrison to man them drove Alderney's population in 1861 to the highest it has ever been – 4932.

The German Occupation

The code name for the Nazi invasion of the Channel Islands was 'Green Arrow'; the code name for the British liberation that ended it was 'Nest Egg'. In between those two military operations, Adolf Hitler ordered that the Channel Islands be made impregnable.

An undefended zone
On 19 June 1940, Channel Islanders learned that their islands, in this war, were no longer seen by the British Government as the first line of defence against the enemy. Worse than that, their islands were not to be defended at all. They were to be completely demilitarised and declared an undefended zone. How had such an incredible situation arisen?

As the German forces in 1940 started their swift advance through Holland, Luxembourg and Belgium, they posed an ever growing threat to France and the British forces fighting there. On 28 May the British troops began their evacuation from France, via Dunkirk.

By the early days of June, the Allies were in full retreat from France and the Germans were approaching the coast of Normandy. Channel Islanders were asking themselves about the future, but few of them could have been prepared for the announcement that the islands were to be left undefended.

One of the many tragic aspects of the affair is that no one in authority told the Germans about the decision to demilitarise the islands, and on 28 June 1940, Heinkel bombers bombed both Guernsey and Jersey, killing a total of 40 people, in the belief that the islands were being defended.

Only on 30 June did the Germans learn otherwise, via the US Embassy in Berlin. It had been feared that an open admission that they were undefended would be tantamount to inviting the Germans to invade. It was and they did, without any opposition, on 1 July 1940.

Different experiences
The German Occupation affected each of the Channel Islands differently. Alderney, once demilitarisation had been declared, was almost completely evacuated. The Germans made extensive use of forced labour to turn it into a huge fortress, with massive gun emplacements and a network of underground shelters and tunnels.

The 320 acres of Herm were primarily used to fatten the cattle, sheep and heifers not required in

The German-built steel-lined Command Bunker at Noir Mont, Jersey

A bunker at St Ouen's Bay, Jersey, one of many German-built defences around the bay

Guernsey for breeding purposes. Only in 1942 were two light anti-aircraft gun emplacements constructed there to deter the Allied bombers taking a heavy toll of German shipping in St Peter Port.

Except for an 11-week occupation by the troops needed to fire the guns, Guernseyman F M Dickson and his wife looked after Herm, with only two and then three other couples.

In Sark, Dame Sybil Hathaway declared, when demilitarisation was announced, 'We stay and see this island through'. The Sercquiaise did – all 471 of them. Dame Sybil Hathaway's fluent German helped, and today one of the only reminders of the Occupation is a café, once a German block house.

After evacuation, Guernsey and Jersey were left with populations of about 22,000 and 40,000 respectively. Their different experiences were mainly due to the different temperaments of the German commandants in charge of each island, and to the characters of the Bailiffs who had to deal with them, Victor Carey in Guernsey and Alexander Coutanche in Jersey.

The three German officers in overall command of the Channel Isles during the Occupation were Major-General Muller, Colonel Graf von Schmettow and Vice-Admiral Hoffmeier. The men under them were not, on the whole, fanatical Nazis, and they seemed pleased to be out of the strenuous theatre of war in Europe.

For the most part, the relationship between occupied and occupier was good. But life was far from easy. There had been wartime restrictions before the Germans invaded – blackout and restrictions on the use of motor vehicles for example. There had been a curfew since France fell in June 1940; in common with the rest of the British Isles, the islands had also had rationing. These restrictions, though, were as nothing compared with what Channel Islanders had to endure before they were liberated.

Verboten!
Every day it seemed the Germans were posting up a new 'order'. These were all 'to be strictly obeyed'. They ranged from the prohibition of spirits through to such re-organising as the putting forward to Central European time of all clocks and watches; the transferring of traffic from left to right; and switching from sterling to Reichsmarks. Certain areas were designated military zones and were *verboten*. The order which bit hardest was perhaps that issued in June 1942 – all wireless sets belonging to the civilian population had to be handed to the Germans. The order which had the most lasting effect on the face of the islands, however, was that the Channel Islands be turned,

over eight years, into an impregnable fortress.

This job was given to the Organisation Todt, a group of architects and other specialists formed by the brilliant autobahn engineer Dr Fritz Todt. The manual labourers were prisoners of war and civilians that the Germans had collected en route through Europe. The first 'slave' workers came from Franco's Spain (they had backed the 'wrong' side in the Civil War). They were followed by political prisoners from Poland and Czechoslovakia and Jews from Alsace. Worst treated of all these 'slaves' were the Russian POWs, written off by the Germans as *untermenschen* (undermen). All were put to work by the engineers on such major projects as coastal fortifications and the two underground hospitals, in Guernsey and Jersey.

Like island defenders before them, the Germans took fortifications that were already there and added to and thereby improved them for their own purposes. In Alderney, of the 19th-century forts only Les Hommeaux Florains and Houmet Herbé were not strengthened for use; in Guernsey, Fort Saumarez and La Prévôté were typical examples; in Jersey many of the coastal towers, such as Fort William, were utilised.

Among the multitude of Occupation fortifications which are still part of the skyline are Alderney's fire control tower on the outskirts of St Anne, and Guernsey's anti-tank walls bordering L'Ancresse and Vazon. Jersey not only had gun emplacements such as Noir Mont Point but also control towers as at La Corbière. As well as the tanks, the searchlights, the radar equipment, there were also the unseen defences – the mines. From Sark alone

Occupied St Helier – the Forum Cinema

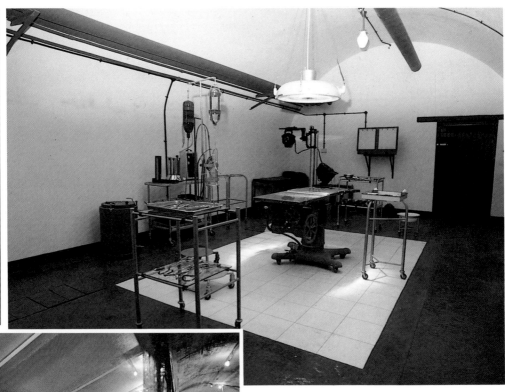

German Military Underground Hospital, Jersey

An Occupation display in the German Military Underground Hospital, St Andrew's, Guernsey

13,000 were cleared after the war.

The Channel Islands were the most heavily fortified area in Western Europe, and the sweep of the German artillery, including Guernsey's powerful Mirus battery, covered the French coast from Cherbourg to Cap Frehel. After D-Day, when British forces were back on French soil, attempts were made to silence the Guernsey and Alderney guns, with some success. D-Day, however, did not bring the immediate liberation of the Channel Isles, as had been so desperately hoped. Rather did the gradual Allied occupation of France by-pass the Channel Isles and, by cutting vital supply lines from Europe, bring greater hardship to both occupiers and occupied than they had ever known in the previous four years.

Rations

The weekly rations in Jersey are typical of the little the Channel Islanders had to eat during the autumn of 1944. Bread: adults 4½lb, children 3lb. Potatoes: 5lb. Breakfast meal: 7oz. Butter: 2oz. Salt: 1oz. Sugar: 3oz (double for a child). Milk: ½pt (double for a child). Medicine, soap, cereals, sugar and salt were running out fast, and by the end of September 1944 were urgently needed.

Many were the devices to eke out the meagre allowance of food and fuel, and to get new clothes. Complete suits were made out of blankets, shoes from wood or bicycle tyres. Sawdust was used for cooking fuel, potatoes for flour, seaweed for a kind of blancmange. Yet, despite the brave making-do, the yearning for food and warmth was constant.

So severe were the restrictions on essential supplies such as gas, electricity and fuel, so short the rations, that the Bailiffs of Guernsey and Jersey begged Churchill to lift the British blockade which was causing such hardship. His reply was adamant: 'I am entirely opposed to our sending any rations to the Channel Islands ostensibly for the civil population but, in fact, enabling the German garrison to prolong their resistance.'

As there were 28,500 German troops and 62,000 civilians, and only enough food to last until January, the two Bailiffs then asked the British and German governments if they might approach the Red Cross. The result was that the Swedish ship, the *Vega*, was loaded with food, medicine and other necessary supplies in Lisbon and reached the islands just after they had lived through their most miserable and deprived Christmas – in near starving conditions – of the war.

Victory

Not for another five months did the Allied victory in Europe become certain, but on 8 May 1945 Churchill was able to broadcast the words that no Channel Islander who heard them will ever forget: '. . . and our dear Channel Islands are also to be freed today'.

After five years of preparing for a British invasion by arming the islands up to the hilt, the besieged Germans capitulated without one shot being fired. The liberation of the Channel Islands was bloodless.

Further information about fortifications and whether they are open to the public can be had by applying to Alderney Museum, St Anne, Alderney; Guernsey Museum, Candie Gardens, St Peter Port, Guernsey; and Jersey Museum, Pier Road, St Helier, Jersey. See also the Directory, page 76, for more information on museums.

Natural History

The Channel Islands are on the tip of a finger pointing at Britain from the Mediterranean Sea. Along it, mild weather conditions, brought about by the warm water of the North Atlantic Drift, allow tender fauna and flora normally associated with southern Europe to enjoy a foothold. The finger lies along the Atlantic seaboard of Spain, Portugal and France, ending at the archipelago of eight populated Channel Islands.

Of the Channel Islands species which are seldom or never found in mainland Britain, Dartford warblers nest in the gorse banks, green lizards have conquered some castles in the islands, loose-flowered orchids turn old wet meadows purple in spring, while the sea is home to ormers – large molluscs which are a local delicacy. Mole crickets make their strident sounds in the sandy soils, Glanville fritillary butterflies skip over the sea cliffs, and holm oaks turn their backs on winter gales to face the warmer climes of their native southern Europe.

It would be reasonable to assume that the Channel Islands have similar wildlife but, although they have things in common, it is the differences between the islands which make them fascinating. Magpies breed in Guernsey and Jersey, but are rare vagrants in Alderney, for example. The local elm, known throughout the UK as the Jersey elm, is common only in Guernsey, and bears the name *Ulmus sarniensis* to mark the fact. Sarnia, meaning green land, is traditionally said to be the old Roman name for Guernsey.

Mammals and other vertebrates are not well represented. The largest wild mammal is the rabbit, which was introduced into all the islands, as was the red squirrel to Jersey, where it thrives. Hedgehogs, slow-worms and frogs abound, although the former were introduced into Sark only recently. Toads and newts are found in Jersey, while moles are in all the islands except Herm and Guernsey.

Jersey's north coast cliffs offer protection to many birds and plants

The anomalies in the distribution of fauna and flora arise from major differences in the geology, the islands' different shapes and the use to which the land is put. Much of this is dependent on the position of each island's cliffs – those in Sark surround its flat plateau on all sides, Jersey's cliffs are in the north so that the island slopes to the south, while the opposite is the case in Guernsey and Herm. Alderney's cliff tops are to the west and south – the main part of the island faces France, so that it has little shelter and a windswept appearance.

All these different positions produce marked contrasts between the climates on the respective islands, in turn influencing the natural history. But another critical factor which has governed what lives where is when the land bridges between the various islands and the French mainland were severed. It occurred early enough to prevent toads and moles from reaching Guernsey, although they are found in Jersey, and green lizards certainly made the crossing.

The need for fuel has also influenced the landscape of the islands, and the things living on them. Until coal became widely available, Islanders cut down anything which grew and a furze brake on the cliffs was part of every farm's property, providing a source of fuel. Prints from old books show the islands almost devoid of trees, but today the fashion of planting them is rife and the islands are becoming greener and more sheltered.

The jacket of water which surrounds the Channel Islands keeps them almost frost free, and the sea's rise and fall (more than 40ft on the highest spring tides) produces large areas of beach where marine biologists (and small children!) can study. The extremely high tides are dangerous, however, and great care should be taken when on the beach. These expanses produce conditions which favour marine creatures and seaweeds, while the clean currents of water which rush past ensure that the beaches are largely unaffected by pollution.

Enigmatic places

Islands are mysterious, enigmatic places on which things happen without apparent reason. This is particularly so with spring and autumn bird migrations, during which the Channel Islands fill with birds overnight and lose them as quickly. They are on the main bird migration routes and act as huge transport cafés for these smallest of long distance travellers. They are also havens for

wintering birds, which make use of the wide range of habitats on land and water.

Birds are not the only creatures which migrate to the islands. Butterflies and moths from southern areas arrive in profusion when the weather is suitable. Clouded yellow, red admiral and peacock butterflies all arrive in mid-summer, and if the south-easterly winds needed are kind, then the spectacular hummingbird hawk moth can be found sipping from honeysuckle and valerian.

Marshland

In the Channel Islands, as in the rest of Britain, marshland is under great pressure from man. There are constant demands for further drainage, pollution from streams running off farmland and destruction of the habitat by modern agricultural techniques. Marshes are becoming increasingly uncommon in the Channel Islands, but where they occur they are rich and productive habitats for plants, birds and insects.

Jersey's biggest marsh is in Les Quennevais and Les Mielles conservation area – set aside by the island's government as a huge nature reserve. Run by La Société Jersiase, St Ouen's Pond, or La Mare au Seigneur as it is sometimes called, is a major bird migration site and provides wintering quarters for wildfowl. It is the largest naturally occurring stretch of open water in the Channel Islands. Surrounded by reedbeds, which are frequently hunted by passing marsh harriers, it has the distinction of providing the first nest site for Cetti's warbler in the British Isles – the nest is now in the Jersey Museum. Grouville Marsh contrasts with the reeds of St Ouen's as it is a grazed and partly wooded area which provides the only Channel Island breeding sites for great and lesser spotted woodpeckers.

Guernsey has a number of marshes formed by floodwater which runs off the inland escarpment along the west coast, and is blocked as it comes up against huge shingle and sandbanks thrown up by the sea. Many of these small marshes have been drained over several hundred years, but all the areas are still wet and in those where traditional farming techniques are used the fields are home to thousands of loose-flowered orchids, *Orchis laxiflora*. They are called the Whitsun orchid in the local French patois, because they turn the fields purple at that time of year. La Société Guernesiaise, which has taken on the role of a county naturalists' trust in Guernsey and is affiliated to the Royal Society for Nature Conservation, owns a number of the fields in the Rue des Vicheries and L'Erée areas of St Peter's.

Another area under their management is the Colin McCathie Nature Reserve at the Vale Pond. The pond is brackish – it is part of an area of land reclaimed in 1805 and is linked by pipe to the sea – but fresh water flowing into it allows the growth of a wide reed bed. The Vale Pond is a magnet for birds at most times of the year, and in particular during the migrations. A hide, with access close to a public car park at Grande Havre, overlooks the pond. At high tide the sea backs up the pipe, covering the mud flats which normally stretch away from the base of the hide. This often takes a while to happen and there is a lag between the tide rising and the mud flats being covered. During this time waders, pushed off the beaches by the tide, drop in to feed. Common, green and wood sandpipers and the usual range of waders found on the beaches, dunlin, ringed plover and redshank,

Top: the clouded yellow butterfly
Bottom: Orchis laxiflora (the 'Whitsun orchid') turns fields purple in summer

can be seen. In winter the pond teems with birds, including scores of snipe, duck (often followed by peregrine), water rail, moorhens and coot.

Guernsey's other major marsh, La Claire Mare at L'Erée, has recently been bought by La Société Guernesiaise and plans are being drawn up for a wader scrape and hide to be built on the site. The society are moving slowly with their planning to ensure that nothing is done to harm the indigenous wildlife.

Herm and Sark have no marshes, but a small pond surrounded by reeds on Alderney's Longis

Right: marsh harrier – a low-flying hunter of the reed-beds. This one is female, with pale crown and throat

Below: La Mare au Seigneur, Jersey, winter quarters for numerous wildfowl

Below left: hummingbird hawk moths arrive on summer south-east winds

Below right: the yellow horned poppy blooms in the fragile habitat of mobile dunes

Common attracts an excellent cross-section of birds. Like the other marshes mentioned, the pond is best observed during migration. Access is easy and the site has birds not normally associated with marshes on the common land around it. Wheatear, whinchat and redstart can often be watched as reed and sedge warblers sing in the pond's margins.

Sand dune grassland

This is one of the most delicate and interesting habitats in the Channel Islands. The lime-rich but dry soils are also a fine contrast to the islands' other land habitats, which are derived from the granite base rock and tend to be acid. Most sand dune grasslands have become established since the

last ice cap retreated – some are no older than 100 years or so – but this development is countered by erosion and by people. Golf courses have been built in the prime sites, while sand has been removed for building or to remove obstructions.

Mobile dunes are found at Saye Bay, Braye and Longis, Alderney, and along the northern coast of Herm. Most mobile dunes in the other islands were protected by sea walls built over the last 125 years and completed in concrete by the Germans during World War II. They are fragile habitats occupied by marram grass, sea holly, yellow horned poppy and sea spurge.

In Guernsey, the common at L'Ancresse is protected by a German wall and the sandy habitat

The mole cricket (left) and Dartford warbler – rare in mainland Britain but common here

has been 'improved' by the creation of a heavily fertilised golf-course. But away from the fairways red fescue and other grasses, kept short by rabbits, thrive, along with scores of tiny plants which induce the familiar 'bottoms in the air' approach to their study by botanists. The area is common land so that golfers have not only the usual hazards of bunkers and gorse patches, but also the botanists, twitchers' tripods and farmers' tethered cattle to put up with. All the different groups use the area in harmony, however. The Common's sandy soil is home to one of Britain's rarest invertebrates, the mole cricket. These ugly but fascinating creatures emerge after dark to rattle their love songs. Sometimes they occur in such numbers that greenhouse crops are damaged by them.

Herm's rabbit population is so large that wire fences have been put around the farmland, keeping the animals on the cliffs and common where they work to the advantage of delicate plants such as lichens and minute specimens of early forget-me-not, burk's-horn plantain and rue-leaved saxifrage, which are nibbled short and protected from the encroachment of stronger plants. The common's limy base can be seen where it meets the sea at Shell Beach. Hundreds of shells, said to have been washed to the island from America by the Gulf Stream and North Atlantic Drift, can be found across the beach. There are fewer now than 30 years ago but pockets of shells can be found on other beaches around the northern part of the island. Les Mielles and Les Quennevais conservation area in Jersey is in many ways like a miniature British National Park. The area has an information centre, Kempt Tower, overlooking St Ouen's Bay. It is a converted Martello tower and won Civic Trust awards when opened in 1985. The area, which is between Val de la Mare Reservoir and St Ouen's Bay, has extensive permanent and moving sand dunes. Of more than 400 specialised plants found there, 16 species, mostly of southern European or Mediterranean origin, are recorded in the *British Red Data Book* as being endangered. Burnet rose, with its white flowers, is one of the species which

link Les Quennevais, L'Ancresse and Herm Common.

Alderney's sand dunes often march into the Seaview and Diver's bars in Braye Street, which is built on, and backs on to, ancient beach heads. They are mobile dunes, although many are well colonised by marram and other grasses, including sea bindweed. Other sand dune grasslands can be found at Saye Bay and the eastern end of Longis (or Longy) Bay where the sand blows around a huge concrete seawall built by the Germans during the Occupation. Longis Common was formed by sand blowing off the beach and has now stabilised to form permanent dune habitat.

Sea cliffs

Covered in gorse, bracken and bramble, these are the greatest scenic glory of the Channel Islands and home to the rare Dartford warbler in the three largest islands. Rabbits keep much of the rank vegetation in check and the cliffs become wild rock gardens with thrift and sea campion, sheep's bit and ox-eye daisies, broom and stonecrop flowering in May and June. Speckled wood butterflies, normally seen in glades within woodland, flit around the treeless cliffs to the amazement of visiting entomologists. They are joined by their sophisticated cousin, the Glanville fritillary, in July. These beautiful insects emerge after a spring spent as black, hairy, red-headed larvae which feed on plaintain. Only plantain found within about 200 yards of the cliff top will do: why this should be is not known.

The headlands of La Moye and Noir Mont in Jersey are baked by the sun in summer, so that the thin acid soil dries, leaving the cliffs burned and bare until the heather blooms in late summer, and autumn squill covers the ground with curly leaves after flowering. Jersey's north coast provides the highest cliffs in the islands. The damp gullies on the shaded coast are filled with water dropwort, hemp agrimony and brambles, made interesting by the presence of woodland species such as lent lilies, bluebells and wood sorrel.

Guernsey's cliffs stretch from St Peter Port to Pleinmont Point, 16 miles of natural nature reserve. The first section to Jerbourg faces east and has shelter from the prevailing wind. It is home to

Sea-cliffs are the home of the Glanville fritillary, seen in summer

Up to 18in long, the green lizard moves lightning-fast

pale house sparrows which are common on the island appear in neighbouring Guernsey for the winter.

Essex Castle in the east and Fort Tourgis in the west mark the two ends of Alderney's cliff walk. They are at their best in spring and early summer, when the flora is set off by blue seas over which white gannets fly, dominating the bird life of the island. They started nesting during the German Occupation, and two colonies, each with about 1900 pairs of birds, can be seen from the cliffs. Giffoine Point, on the south-west corner, is the most dramatic observation point, with views, sounds and even the smell of the colony on Les Etacs reaching the birdwatcher. Observers become the observed, too, as fulmars rise up the cliffs to watch birdwatchers!

Seashore

The sea gives the Channel Islands a natural buffer against many of the problems with which people conserving other areas have to cope. Pollution is minor and rare, although the threat is always present, particularly from the millions of tons of shipping which pass the islands as they enter and leave the English Channel. The island authorities in both Jersey and Guernsey are looking at ways to set up marine nature reserves on which such activities as bait digging and fishing for ormers will be banned.

Many of the bays have very gentle slopes which produce vast areas in which a wide range of sea creatures can be found. These beaches are often swarming with birds. Waders are present for most of the year, with ringed plover and oystercatcher nesting. Vast flocks of other species arrive in July and August on their way to wintering quarters. They are joined by Brent geese which build up to flocks of about 1000 birds in Jersey and 150 in Herm and Guernsey. Red-breasted merganser, scoter and eider, the great northern diver and flocks of great crested grebe appear to the delight of birdwatchers. Visiting birdwatchers are often surprised to see grey heron and kingfisher feeding in the rock pools and on the edge of the tide.

Finally, the sea itself: Braye and Longis beaches in Alderney are the best for marine wildlife with St Aubin's and St Ouen's bays in Jersey, Grande Havre, Vazon, Rocquaine in Guernsey and the east coast of Herm. All are characterised by the presence of edible crabs (known as chancres in the islands) and spider crabs, which are also eaten. The fishing off island shores is excellent, with good runs of bass, mullet and in the sandy bays flatfish, while headlands provide opportunities for catching mackerel and garfish.

the green lizard which grows up to 18in long. The vegetation in the 'Pine Forest', little more than a handful of pines, grows down to the splash zone of the sea, a characteristic shared by Belcroute and Anne Port in Jersey, which also face east. The south coast of Guernsey is windswept, and the cliffs reflect the fact, with prostrate broom and trees which have been decapitated if they dared to put their heads above cover. Kaffir (or hottentot) fig, introduced from South Africa, has a stronghold on some of the most inaccessible parts of the cliffs, carried there by nesting gulls.

Herm's south coast cliffs are similar to Guernsey's, except that between April and July puffins can often be seen bobbing on the water at the base of some of them. Fulmars nest on the ledges along with ravens – species found breeding in all the Channel Islands. Whitethroats and lesser whitethroats scratch out their songs in the undergrowth while pheasants introduced to the island croak their reply from the fields behind the cliffs.

Sark is skirted with cliffs, so much so that waders, which like sandy and muddy shores on which to feed, are rare. Access to the cliff tops is good in most places, thanks to the man who has the mammoth job of cutting back the vegetation along the paths. The windswept plateau of Sark empties of birds at the end of the autumn and the

Islanders Today

Jersey, Guernsey, Alderney, Sark and Herm – each of the five main islands has its own character and none is quite like any other. But Channel Islanders have always had certain basic ways of earning a living in common. The traditional ways are the growing of crops and the raising of cattle. In the 19th century came tourism, while the increasingly attractive money-earner of today is finance. But whatever their livelihood, in whichever island, there has always been a strong tradition for Islanders to 'give something back', reflecting the sturdy independence and community spirit of all the Channel Islands people.

The Senator – Jersey

Jersey's equivalent of Chancellor of the Exchequer, for its over 80,000 residents, almost a million visitors a year and over fifty banks, is the President of the island's Finance and Economics Committee, Senator Reg Jeune. In his 24 years in the States (the equivalent of Parliament), Senator Jeune has also been President of the Public Works and Education Committees and (since these are all part-time honorary offices) has combined his work in the States with being a solicitor of the Royal Court. He is also a director of several companies and earned an OBE for his long period of service with the Trustee Savings Bank.

The demands of one day may be many and various. 'At 9.15 last Monday, as Vice-President of the Legislation Committee, I was discussing such matters as Jersey's constitution and the way in which EEC regulations impinge on the island. Then from 12 to 2, over a sandwich lunch, we had a TSB meeting. A Finance and Economics meeting took the whole afternoon until 6.30, discussing

Jersey Senator Reg Jeune

subjects like land transactions and the Regulation of Undertakings Law – which ensures that anyone who wants to enlarge their business or start up a new one, has to have our approval. It's one of our tools in this island for controlling immigration.'

Tuesday is States day in Jersey. Senator Jeune attended a Defence Committee meeting on traffic before the States started, and chaired a board meeting in the evening. Lunch was spent at an American bank, listening to a talk on world economics. Wednesday began with a press conference on the draft of the new Jersey Company Law (to replace one 125 years old), followed at 11.30 by a Treasury meeting with officers from Customs and Excise, Income Tax, Commercial Relations, the Economic Advisor and the Treasurer of the States. 'We had an important preliminary discussion about the forthcoming November budget.' All day Thursday Senator Jeune was in London for the monthly meeting of the TSB.

'Being President of Finance is a monumental job. Almost everything in the States, if it involves expenditure, comes to the Committee of Finance and Economics. Whether it's housing, education, the airport, the hospital – whatever, it all has to come for our approval or otherwise.'

Jersey's States (parliament) Chamber, St Helier

*Members' entrance to the States Chamber,
St Helier*

The biggest contributor to Jersey's economy is the finance industry: 50 banks and numerous finance houses have made their base on the island, attracted by the guiding policy of Presidents of Finance for many decades.

'Income tax in Jersey is at 20 per cent, which my predecessors and I would never change. So we cut our cloth accordingly. In any one year we look at the size of the financial cake and we divide it into three main slices: one goes to reserves, the second to revenue expenditure – for the day-to-day running of the island – and the third to capital expenditure.

'Our problem is one that nine-tenths of the rest of the world would like – we in Jersey have a booming economy! But that means that there's a great demand for expansion – which means more building, which could eventually spoil this lovely island. We are trying to keep the balance between prosperity on the one hand, and safeguarding the island from being spoiled on the other.'

Senator Jeune has the best reasons for wanting to safeguard Jersey. His Huguenot ancestors fled here in the 16th century, and it is the Jerseyman of several generations who has the last word. 'My own policy is this: my island is a lovely one and I intend to keep it that way. That's why I work so hard in the States.'

The farmer – Guernsey

Most of Mr Herbert Martel's 81 years have been devoted to caring for Guernsey cattle. When talking about his land, he uses the Norman land measure, the *vergée* – 1960sq yd in Guernsey and 2151sq yd in Jersey.

'I moved into Border Farm in 1932 when I got married. In its thirty *vergées* I started off with fifteen cows and six heifers and never went above sixteen cows. The way I look at it is, what you have, you've got to look after properly. And as I've always hand-milked my cows, that was what I could manage.'

Like their Jersey counterparts, Guernseys are traditionally tethered to one spot of grazing with a long rope. Unlike them, they do not wear green tarpaulin jackets to protect them from the weather. 'I once told a Jersey farmer when I saw his cows with their coats on, you want to breed something a bit more hardy than that!' Nevertheless, he followed the traditional Channel Island way and always brought his cows in during the winter nights.

He began helping on the family farm at the age of six. 'I would get up before six o'clock, help milk the cows, then go with my father in his pony and trap delivering the milk to our 200 customers. At 8.55 punctually my father would drop me outside the school.'

He kept the habit of early rising throughout his long farming career. 'By breakfast at eight, the cows would have been fed, milked – the first delivery was collected at eight – and they and the young stock given their final feed. At 8.30 I'd muck out the stables and in the winter I'd have the stables ready and their feed out for their coming in early in the afternoon.'

'At 12.15 sharp my wife, who was always ready to work with me on any of the jobs, would have my lunch ready. Then I'd go out and move the tethers of the cows for fresh grazing. The longer the hours of daylight, the longer I'd be able to leave the cows out and get on with the growing of

Guernsey farmer Herbert Martel

all their foodstuffs – the kale, mangolds, hay.

'The afternoon milk delivery came at 5.30, so after a cup of tea at 3.30 there was the second milking to do. Then, except at haymaking, I made sure I got everything done by six o'clock. Twelve hours a day was enough.'

It was 20 years before the Martels had a break from the farm. 'Even then we had to go away separately; it wasn't until ten years later we had our first holiday away together.'

Two years before Mr Martel retired from farming in 1974, he started to serve in the government of Guernsey – the States. 'I first went into the States against my will, because of the farm, but once I'd taken on a youngster from school I had more time. In fact, over the years I trained three such youngsters, and they're all now in business on their own.'

Despite the reluctant start, he eventually sat on no fewer than seven different States committees. A natural choice for the Agricultural – he served as its President from 1982-1985 – and Horticultural Committees, he was also President of Guernsey's

Beau Sejour Leisure Centre for six of its formative years, from 1979-1985. One of his best cows, Princess Sheila of the Border, was the mother of the first bull used by the Artificial Insemination Centres, so it is appropriate that he was also on the AI Committee. He became one of the two judges who inspect all bulls in Guernsey for AI – a job which carries a very great responsibility for the future of the Guernsey breed.

Mr Martel has sold the farming land of Border Farm to his nephew, but has only rented him his cows. So he still sees his own herd coming down the road from his nephew's farm, and can watch them graze where his cows have grazed since he started farming in this corner of Guernsey all those years ago.

Ready for court, Alderney Jurat George Baron

The Jurat – Alderney

Jurat Baron's family came to Alderney in the 1850s, as builders and contractors employed by the British Government to construct its answer to France's new naval base in Cherbourg, 'a harbour of refuge and observation' in Alderney. Over 100 years later and 22 years ago the family firm was still engaged in building – helping restore Alderney after the German Occupation – when George Baron was made a Jurat. This is an honorary position, not known outside the Channel Islands, 'but it's somewhat equivalent,' says Jurat Baron, 'to UK magistrates and Crown Court judges.

'In the court of Alderney there are seven jurats, selected from island residents and appointed by the Crown, who remain in office until they're 70. None of us need come from a legal background but we're helped by the Clerk of the Court who will normally have had a training in law.'

Until 1976, he was also President of the States of Alderney. 'But after six years as President, I had to decide which office I wanted to hold, because it was thought best to separate the judiciary from the civil administration. In the event I elected to remain a jurat.'

As a jurat, he has to observe several traditional customs when he goes to court. These all date back to the time when the Channel Islands were part of the Duchy of Normandy and the laws were based on 'Le Grand Coutumier de Normandie'. Jurats wear a gown and hat of Norman origin; at the opening and closing of each sitting the prayers are in French; what is more, so are many of the island's laws. Even the 1894 Alderney Company Law, with which present-day companies have to comply, has never been translated into English.

'But Alderney can claim one first. Since the war, conveyancing of real estate, unlike in the other islands, is no longer under the system of French contracts. Nowadays we have a central land registry where conveyances can be completed at 48 hours' notice.'

What sort of cases come before the court? 'Some of the old island families still use litigation to settle matters of honour and pride, but the cost is increasingly a deterrent. Most of our civil cases range from matrimonial to property, with a decline in litigation over debt and an increase in more complicated civil matters involving external business being administered through our company laws. In fact, just now more immediate controls are being legislated for in the banking and finance sectors.

'Criminal cases are mainly restricted to motoring offences. Serious crime is very rare, and we have very little vandalism.'

Being a jurat is not, however, his sole involvement in island affairs. 'Alderney is still suffering from the effects of the war – it was completely evacuated right at the beginning of the war and only 25 per cent of the old families returned – which means it has the lowest percentage of indigenous population in the whole of the Channel Isles. So I've been interested in any matter that improves the social life of the community – I was a founder member of the island's sailing club and its golf club, for instance.'

Despite the satisfaction he finds in his involvement with island life, he is concerned about Alderney's future. As the father of six children and thirteen grandchildren, none of whom lives in Alderney, he has first-hand experience of what he sees as its biggest problem.

'My main anxiety is the ever-growing age gap between young and old. Many people who retire to Alderney have a great deal to give to the island, but it doesn't bode well when our young people leave to get further education on the mainland, or to find scope for their energies which they can't find here, and perhaps don't come back until they themselves retire. My fear is that Alderney could eventually become an island without young people.'

The Post Office Clerk – Sark

No cramped commuting for those who work in Sark. It takes Belinda Adams only five minutes to cycle from her home on the island's east coast for her nine o'clock start as assistant in Sark's one and only post office. The post office is also a general stores, so its counters are crammed full of necessities for Serquiaise and visitors alike.

'In the summer, as soon as I arrive, I stock up on our post cards – the ones that go fastest are the aerial view of Sark and Grand Grève beach by the Coupée – and then clean, dust and tidy up in between serving early customers. We sell petrol by the gallon for the tractors, builders' materials, gardening equipment and kitchen hardware for the locals, with souvenirs like Sark tea towels and pens for visitors.'

On the postal side, Sark's post office is a branch of Guernsey's, and sells only Guernsey stamps. In the 1986 season these included the definitive sets of Sark's La Coupée, which played such a dramatic part in the TV series, *Mr Pye*, and its Seigneurie. The hand-stamped Sark cancellation is much sought after and prized by philatelists.

'The mail usually arrives by boat from Guernsey about 11 o'clock. Some people collect their mail from here; others wait for it to be delivered. Outgoing mail has to be sorted into Guernsey, English and foreign by 9.30 and 4.30 in the summer and an hour before the boat goes in winter – it varies because of the weather.'

At one o'clock, like most of Sark's other shop assistants, Belinda cycles home for lunch and does not have to be back until two, and in the slack winter period, the post office only stays open for four afternoons.

Belinda's parents, with whom she lives, are engaged in two traditional mainstays of Channel Island life – fishing and tourism. 'My father fishes mostly for lobsters, spider crabs and chancres – most of them he sells to the hotels here and the rest to Guernsey. He's out eight or nine hours at a time – sometimes he gets up at four o'clock to catch the tide. My mother takes the money at the gate of the Seigneurie and helps out at one or two of the shops when they're busy.

'Father was Constable of Sark, and then he was elected eight years ago as Deputy on the Chief Pleas, which is the island parliament; and mother is Sark's first ever woman churchwarden, in our St Peter's Church.'

What is it like for a young girl to live in tiny,

Miss Belinda Adams, postal clerk on Sark

car-less Sark? 'In the summer I always go to the discos every Tuesday and Saturday at the Mermaid and meet the people there – mainly seasonal hotel staff. I get my clothes from Guernsey or from catalogues – there are really none in Sark for my age group – and then I have to go to Guernsey for records and tapes.'

In winter, there are amateur theatricals. 'The Sark Theatre Group rehearse once a week. Last year I had three small parts in *The Big Noise at Fortissimo*. We could get the plays ready in a much shorter time but we like to wait until March for the production, then we put it on at the Island Hall for two or three nights and most of the Islanders come to see it. It's really like a social evening all through the winter, an excuse to get out, and the producer chooses plays to fit in as many as possible of the people who are interested.'

'Yes, it can get a bit quiet at times in Sark. I have thought about going away at some point, just to see what it's like. I think it's a good idea for Islanders to get away. But I'll always come back.'

The name Belinda Adams might seem familiar to gardeners: her grandmother, a member of the Geranium Society, bred a new variety and named it after her.

Left: Sark's hand-franking stamp. Right: a post box on Sark

General Manager Adrian Heyworth – never far from home on Herm's 400 acres

The Island Manager – Herm

Adrian Heyworth is General Manager of an island – the 400 acres which make up Herm.

Herm is owned by Guernsey, where Mr Heyworth was born, but its present tenants, with a lease running until 2029, are the Wood family, whose responsibility it is to see to the upkeep of everything above the high water mark. This is now the duty of Adrian Heyworth who married into the family – his wife is Pennie, the third of the Wood children and the first baby to be born in Herm for a hundred years.

'I have to run a successful, high turnover business, whose governing principle is that Herm must be commercial but must not appear to be commercialised. The running costs are about £150,000 a year, with no support from Guernsey.'

Herm is also home for nine other families and to keep it commercially viable, Adrian Heyworth, qualified in estate management, must be prepared to do anything and everything.

'I rise at seven sharp for a family breakfast with Pennie and my two young children. We value this time together. Then, before 8am, I make any phone calls to tradespeople in Guernsey we may need. Then I see to our own maintenance team of four and allocate them their jobs for the day. Next, to the truck drivers – who have to go round to the litter bins and loos – to make sure that all is OK, and to see that the surplus milk from our own 100-strong Guernsey herd is ready to be shipped to Guernsey by nine.'

'When the first ferry boat from Guernsey comes in, I'm always there to meet it and help with the manhandling of anything up to ten tons of provisions for the trading departments. My administration office is down on the harbour and, as the paperwork is the part of my job I don't like, I'm very ruthless and very fast during the hour or two I spend there, delegating as much as I can to my excellent secretary. We're fortunate in also having a chartered accountant on the island.

'Next, I see every manager and trading department on the island, including the beach cafés. Our season is short, so everything has got to be right. There's also a meeting of top management once a month, because part of my job is troubleshooting and making sure that standards are maintained, as well as peace and tranquillity. We are also great conservationists.

'From eleven I'm free to do what I want.' Up to a point. Today he has basic maintenance jobs at the campsite – giving him an opportunity to chat to the campers. Yesterday he was salvaging a French yacht shipwrecked on the rocks. Tomorrow could be what he calls a 'smart day', when he talks to journalists for the promotion of the island, or when Herm is hosting a large conference lunch, at which the presence of the manager would be expected. Afterwards, he could find himself at the sink, helping with the washing up.

But all these jobs are done in an island only one and a half miles long and half a mile wide, and it is a source of great satisfaction that he never finds himself far from home.

'I can see my wife and children throughout the day. My kids understand what Daddy does, because they see me doing it. I'm back home by six, so I can help put them to bed.'

By then the day is far from finished for their father. 'In the summertime, I put on my jacket and tie and go on duty in the hotel or tavern, chatting to the guests, acting as a special constable, checking who is coming to the island in their private boats – we can choose who we have on our premises, and no one can be on Herm after sunset without permission.'

Catering plays an important part on the island, so Adrian and Pennie Heyworth like to dine in the restaurant two or three times a week. It gives them a chance to meet the guests, and dining and wining done, it is Mr Heyworth's responsibility to see that Herm's guests leave the island safely – and quietly, so as not to spoil the peaceful night atmosphere.

The day's work might not be over until 11.30 – but for Herm's manager the good life is one which combines physical and mental work – and he believes he is living it.

The Seas Around the Islands

The Channel Islands are ringed by coastlines of great beauty, vivid contrasts and surprising extent. Guernsey has 25 miles of coast, Jersey has 20 miles of beaches alone, and many more of cliffs and rocks. For swimming, sailing, surfing or fishing, the islands are unsurpassed. But for those who know them, these seas are well respected for startlingly swift tides, rising as much as 40ft, for turbulent races, treacherous currents and tempestuous tempers when aroused.

For as long as records go back, the sea has brought the Islanders both wealth and sorrow.

Midnight assassins

Wind and tide meet at their strongest at the Casquets, to the west of Alderney, the first rocks

'The Rescue of the Johan Collet' off St Peter Port. (David Cobb – 1963)

to greet an English visitor to the Channel Islands. Ancient records speak of it as 'this destroying place'. Even after lights had been placed there, Admiral Sir John Balchen's 100-gun *Victory* was wrecked on the rocks, in October 1744, with the loss of every member of its 1000 crew.

Of Guernsey's Hanois Rocks Victor Hugo said 'This rock – this midnight assassin – has filled the cemeteries of Torteval and Rocquaine.' In 1911 on the notorious Les Kaines Rocks, at the western end of St Brelade's Bay, Jersey, the *TSS Roebuck* was

Painting by P J Duless of a wreck off Corbière, Jersey, 1859

shipwrecked one foggy July night and her hundred or so passengers had to take to the boats – fortunately without loss of life.

No wonder then that lighthouses are a distinctive feature of the Channel Isles seascape. Alderney has the 106ft Quesnard lighthouse on its north-eastern point, whose light is visible from 17 miles away. Hanois and the Platte Fougère lighthouses stand to the north and south of Guernsey. Perhaps the most picturesque of all is Jersey's Corbière lighthouse.

This beautiful place has another sad tale to tell, and a salutary warning to give, of the swift inrush of the tides in the Channel Isles. At the entrance to the causeway a stone stands in memory of *'Peter Edwin Larbalestier, assistant keeper at the lighthouse, who on 28 May 1946 gave his life in attempting to rescue a visitor cut off by the incoming tide. Take heed, all ye that pass by!'*

Riches of the sea

Islanders, though, have always enjoyed the challenge of the sea while respecting its power, and over the centuries it has been their livelihood. Several of Guernsey's and Jersey's fine Georgian houses are known as 'cod houses' as they were built with fortunes made in fishing for Newfoundland cod and selling it salted to the Continent. Fishing and other trades, such as the export of granite, from Alderney and Herm as well as the larger islands, led to shipbuilding. This was at its peak in the 19th century, with the main shipyards in Guernsey at Havelet, St Julian's Rock, La Piette, Les Banques and St Sampson, and Jersey's shipyards extending all along the south coast. Even the Lower Park in St Helier was once famed for its shipbuilding.

The Channel Islands were ideally placed for more illicit ways of making a living. Sark, for instance, had become a pirate's base when it was colonised by Helier de Carteret in the 16th century.

Later, the most profitable sea trades for some families were smuggling and privateering (authorised piracy). Fleets from the Channel Islands in the 18th and early 19th centuries drove the Governor of Cherbourg to complain to the French Government that both Guernsey and Jersey were the despair of French shipping as each fresh war broke out.

Edmund Burke declared, however, that the islands were almost entitled to be called 'one of the naval powers of the world'. During the Seven Years War Jersey alone brought home 'prize' enemy ships to the value of £60,000.

Smuggling, or 'free trade', was for long a traditional pastime of Channel Islanders and many were the casks of wine and brandy hidden from His Majesty's Revenue Officers. The caves on Jersey's north coast are typical smugglers' caves, while Jean Allaire, Guernsey's most successful 19th-century smuggler, kept his ill-gotten gains in the vast underground vaults of a large house – now the Lieutenant Governor of Guernsey's official residence.

Today – a wealth of leisure

The coasts which have brought the Channel Islands riches offer a wealth of leisure activities today (though the need to respect the sea has in no way diminished). No visit would be complete without at least one or two bracing *coast walks*. Jersey's north cliff walk stretches from Gros Nez in the west to Bouley Point in the east. Guernsey's cliff

path runs for 16 miles along its southern coast. Private property may drive the walker round Alderney's coast inland from time to time, but Sark and Herm – one with no cars, the other with no roads – are a paradise for those on foot.

Walkers are constantly reminded of the power of the sea, dramatic in the seething waters of Le Gouffre, Guernsey, and the subterranean boilings at the Devil's Hole in Jersey, impressive at the massive opening in the cliffs of Sark's Creux Derrible.

These island cliff walks are also ideal for flower lovers, butterfly spotters and bird-watchers. The steep slopes are carpeted in gorse, heather and changing drapes of hottentot fig, and delicate delights such as speckled wood butterflies and the handsome Glanville fritillary can also be discovered. A wide variety of birds nest on the cliffs.

Solid though they may look, some cliffs are liable to crumble, and climbing should not be attempted except on the advice of the tourist board or coastguard, and with proper equipment and adequate training and experience.

Choosing a beach

Local people know that with a coast on every side to choose from, they will always be able to find a beach which is sheltered from the wind. Choosing a beach for a day by the sea is a matter of finding out where the wind is coming from, and heading in the opposite direction. On Guernsey, for instance, if the wind is driving from the north, Fermain Bay sheltered to the north, is ideal; but if a south-easterly is prevailing, then any bay from sunny L'Ancresse to the fisherman's harbour of Portelet should give shelter.

Left: sunset at St Clement's Bay, Jersey

Right: windsurfers enjoy the warm coastal waters for their exhilarating sport

Bottom left: spectacular views over the sea from the cliff walk at Icart

Bottom right: collecting shells at Shell Beach, Herm

Whatever beach is chosen, remember that the tide rises very fast in these islands: take care not to get cut off. Hidden rocks make it inadvisable to dive in unknown waters, while inflatable toys and airbeds should not be taken into the water as they can easily be carried out to sea by wind and currents. If in any doubt, ask the coastguard or tourist office when and where it is safe to swim.

Good beaches on Alderney include Braye Bay within walking distance of St Anne's, where bathing is safe at all times. Perhaps the most beautiful of Alderney's bays, with fine stretches of sand, are those on the north-east coast, about one and a half miles from town. A bus runs to Corblets, Arch and Saye from Marais Square at regular intervals.

Most renowned of Herm's attractions is the treasure trove of its Shell Beach. The fact that shells are found in such profusion on this island alone is due to the swirling currents and restless tides which surround it.

As well as delightful bathing coves in Sark and caves to explore, Sark has the extra pleasure of the Venus Pool when the tide is out. Twenty-five minutes' walk from La Coupée, this circular rock pool is about 20ft deep, with beautiful clear waters which look most inviting in calm weather.

Sun worshippers tan side by side at St Brelade's Bay, Jersey; or can seek the shelter of a cove at Beauport, or any quiet, little-frequented beach.

Watersports

The five-mile stretch of golden sand of St Ouen's Bay on Jersey's coast, provides some of the best *surfing* in the Channel Islands on its Atlantic rollers, as well as *sand racing*. Schools for beginners in surfing, *windsurfing* and *water-skiing* have been set up in Jersey. The Longboat Windsurfing Centre is in Grouville Bay; the centre for water-skiing lies between La Haule Slipway and Bel Royal in St Aubin's Bay; and tuition for windsurfing can be had in St Brelade's Bay. Hobie-cats, specialised high-speed catamarans, are a feature of St Ouen's Bay.

In Guernsey longboard surfing is restricted to a specific area on Vazon Bay, while for windsurfers, Cobo (where the Prince of Wales learned the sport) and Pembroke beaches have specially designated launching sections.

Permits can be had from the Board of Administration for water-skiing off several of Guernsey's east and south coast bays as well as off Herm's Shell Beach.

Diving gives an opportunity to see wrecks and a rich underwater wildlife. Lessons are available, and there are club outings for those who have already learned. Jersey, Guernsey and Alderney have sub aqua clubs. Newcomers to the islands should not risk the local currents without local expertise.

Fishing is popular in all the islands. Guernsey has been spoken of as a 'sea anglers' paradise' and good sport can be had from either shore or boat. Boats for deep sea fishing can be taken from the bigger harbours.

Those *sailing* to the Channel Islands can moor at Braye Harbour in Alderney, or drop anchor in the Victoria and Albert marinas on Guernsey, or in Jersey's St Helier Harbour. Yachts can be chartered in Jersey and Guernsey. Experience is essential for this but sailing lessons are available for beginners.

Weather, wind and tides

Information on weather and the tides is given daily in the local newspaper, over the local radio or can be had by phoning the local harbour master or coastguard. Danger flags on beaches indicate that any attempt to go in or on the water would be unsafe and must be obeyed.

Those in sight of Jersey's signal station on Fort Regent may even see the storm cones hoisted on one of the few stations left in the British Isles still using a signalling system 150 years old. Christmas and Easter visitors to Jersey can see the signal station's special 40ft high and 30ft wide cross. When lit up at night it can be seen round the island from Grouville to St Aubin and as far out to sea as the southernmost group of rocks that make up the Channel Islands, Les Minquiers.

The Channel Islands are a beautiful natural playground for those who enjoy water sports

CHANNEL ISLANDS

Gazetteer

*Each entry in this Gazetteer has the atlas page number on which the place can be found and its grid reference included under the heading.
An explanation of how to use the grid is given on page 82.*

Above: At the Eric Young Orchid Foundation, Trinity, Jersey

The centrepiece of Jersey's central market – a 15ft-high ornamental fountain

Jersey
St Helier

Map Ref: 86WV6548

It cannot be said that this is a particularly beautiful town, though there are lovely parks, a most attractive enclosed market, historic buildings and VAT-free shopping made easier by the pedestrian precincts.

The Royal Square, site of the Battle of Jersey and for centuries the market place, is now shaded by chestnut trees and watched over by a statue of George II. It is surrounded by historic buildings, including the States Chamber, the old corn market (now a bank) and a military picket house of 1803. Across the road stands the parish church, dedicated to the town's patron saint and founded in the 10th or 11th century.

Howard Davis Park, actually in St Saviour but on the eastern outskirts of the town, is the most spacious and beautiful park. Opened in 1939, it was given to the island by T B Davis in memory of his son, who died in action in 1916. At the opposite end of St Helier, to the west, is People's Park below the wooded slopes of Westmount. This large recreation area includes a children's playground and a funfair is staged here during Battle of Flowers week. The Parade Gardens, to the north of the General Hospital, are situated on the parade-ground built by General Don whose statue now overlooks the gardens.

Above the town is the Fort Regent Entertainment and Sports Centre. Here is surely something for the whole family from swimming, badminton, squash, snooker and trampolines to an adventure play area for toddlers, a funfair and live entertainment. Gloucester Hall, opened in 1978, can be transformed from a sports arena into a 2000-seat auditorium for major concerts, and there are also museums, shops, eating-places and a disco within the complex. Certainly a novel use for a fortress built to defend St Helier at the beginning of the 19th century.

Over one-third of Jersey's population lives in the capital city of St Helier

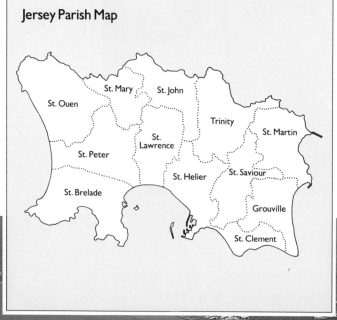

Jersey Parish Map

St. Mary
St. John
St. Ouen
Trinity
St. Martin
St. Lawrence
St. Peter
St. Helier
St. Saviour
St. Brelade
Grouville
St. Clement

Elizabeth Castle

Map Ref: 86WV6347

A great deal of money has recently been spent on a film explaining this vast castle and its chequered history. This captures the mysticism of the hermit, St Helier, living in his cave on L'Islet. It tells of the great Abbey built here in the 12th century, and explains the building of the castle in the late 16th century. Sir Walter Raleigh took up residence in the Governor's House here in 1600, and christened the new castle Fort Isabella Bellissima (Elizabeth the Most Beautiful) after his sovereign. During the reign of Charles I the castle trebled in size, so that by the time of the Civil War it was able to withstand a lengthy siege. Charles II stayed twice at the castle, the first time as a 15-year-old prince and later, in 1649, as proclaimed king, even though the British parliament had abolished the monarchy. The Abbey, along with two-thirds of the castle's provisions and all of its gunpowder, was destroyed in 1651, just as the Governor was preparing for another siege. This meant that the castle, along with the rest of the island, fell to the Parliamentarians. Today, all that remains of the Abbey is a granite cross on the site of the high altar.

It is a good idea to watch the film first, before exploring the castle. There is also an exhibition room, a Militia Museum and a portrait gallery.

The castle can be reached by foot at low tide, or by the commercial amphibious vessels which leave regularly from the West Park slipway.

Top left: The Hermitage stands on an islet south of Elizabeth Castle

Top right: a gun exhibit and tableau in Elizabeth Castle

Bottom: view back to Elizabeth Castle from the causeway

St Helier – The Man

All that is positively known about this holy man who gave his name to Jersey's capital is that he lived a life of prayer, fasting and solitude on a rock now known as the Hermitage, and that he was axed to death by pirates, probably Norsemen, in AD 555. However, as with all these early Christian saints, legends have grown up around him, and it is pleasing to believe that at least some of these are true. We are told he was Belgian, from the town of Tongres, and that his birth was the result of a miracle performed by a missionary, St Cunebert, who then claimed him for God. Helier left Belgium when his father, wanting him back, assassinated St Cunebert. After a brief sojourn in an abandoned chapel in the Cotentin, Helier arrived at the town of Nanteuil, where he was baptised by St Marcoulf, a leading missionary in the area. It was Marcoulf who had apparently introduced Christianity into Jersey around the year 538 and when Helier indicated that he wanted a life of complete seclusion, Marcoulf directed him to the recently converted island. Here, with the help of another saint, Romard, he found what he was looking for on a rock near l'Islet, where Elizabeth Castle now stands. It seems that because of constant raids, there were only 30 inhabitants in the whole of Jersey, all terrified of strangers, but they came to trust this simple man who spent his life in deprivation. St Marcoulf, while visiting the island in 543, witheld a pirate attack by making the sign of the cross, but 12 years later, Helier was not so fortunate. Alone and defenceless, he was hacked to death near his cell by marauding Norsemen.

It is said the tide carried his body to Bréville, a village on the coast of Normandy where he had wished to be buried. This is just feasible, and there is a church dedicated to his name in the village.

To this day, on St Helier's Day, or the Sunday closest to 16 July, a pilgrimage wends its way from the town of his name to the 12th-century oratory built over his cave, and a wreath is laid in his memory.

The crest of the Parish of St Helier is two crossed axes – a stark reminder of this martyr's violent death.

The Jersey Museum

Map Ref: 86WV6548

The museum in Pier Road contains not only some of Jersey's finest art treasures, but also exhibitions depicting life here through the ages.

One of Jersey's most famous daughters was Lillie Langtry, born Emilie Charlotte Le Breton, the daughter of a dean of Jersey, on 13 October 1853. Lillie lived in Jersey until her first marriage to Edward Langtry in 1874 when she moved to England and high society. In her 30s she was forced, for financial reasons, to take up acting. She toured the British Isles, the United States of America and South Africa and became wealthy enough to own racehorses, a ranch in California and a steam yacht. Lady de Bathe, as she became after her second marriage, died in 1929 and was buried in St Saviour's churchyard.

Lillie's beauty and her lifestyle as a close friend of the Prince of Wales and Oscar Wilde, still excite attention, as does the Lillie Langtry Room at the museum. Many of her possessions are on show here, including a quite beautiful travelling case. There are letters and posters from her acting career, and her portrait, painted by Sir Edward Poynter, looks down from the wall. Also exhibited are dresses, made for the television series *Lillie*.

This is just one of many exhibitions in a fascinating and ever-changing museum.

AA recommends:
Hotels: Grand, The Esplanade, 4-star, *tel.* (0534) 22301
Apollo, St. Saviour's Rd, 3-star, *tel.* (0534) 25441
Beaufort, Green St, 3-star, *tel.* (0534) 32471
Pomme D'Or, The Esplanade, 3-star, *tel.* (0534) 78644
Mountview, St John's Rd, 2-star, *tel.* (0534) 78887
Royal Yacht, The Weighbridge, 2-star, *tel.* (0534) 20511
L Hotel Savoy, Rouge Bouillon, 2-star, *tel.* (0534) 27521
Restaurant: La Buca, The Parade, 1-fork, *tel.* (0534) 34283
Guesthouses: Almorah Hotel, La Pouquelaye, *tel.* (0534) 21648
Cliff Court Hotel, St Andrews Rd, First Tower, *tel.* (0534) 34919
Runnymede Court Hotel, 46-52 Roseville St, *tel.* (0534) 20044
Garages: Cleveland, Mont A'L'Abbe, *tel.* (0534) 33233
Colebrooks (CI), 1-2 Victoria St, *tel.* (0534) 37357
Tony Perchard, 13/15 Stopford Rd, *tel.* (0534) 71555

Lillie Langtry's beautiful travelling case – each piece has a solid gold centre engraved 'LL', surrounded with turquoise

The Battle of Jersey

In 1778 France allied itself to the American colonies at war with Britain. All the ancient hostility against Jersey rose to the surface again, and many plans were laid to invade and conquer this tiny British island.

The Baron de Rullecourt was a soldier of fortune who saw his future, if his attack succeeded, as Governor of a French Jersey. He prepared his expedition with care, choosing Twelfth Night for the invasion because the militia were likely to be carousing. It was 11 o'clock on the moonless 6 January of 1781 that de Rullecourt and his men landed undetected and unexpected at La Rocque, after being guided by a traitorous local pilot through the rocks and gulleys that defended the harbour. Leaving a rearguard of 100 men at La Rocque, the Baron marched on St Helier, there waking the Lieutenant-Governor, Major Moise Corbet, and forcing him to sign a capitulation. All might have been over, but for the bravery of the Jersey Militia, the regulars and, in particular, Francis Peirson, a 24-year-old Major in the 95th Regiment. This gallant young officer took charge of the soldiers who had congregated on the slopes of Westmount. He met the Lieutenant-Governor and was not put off by Corbet's entreaties to surrender his forces and deposit their arms in the Royal Court, saying 'We have decided to defend the island for as long as we live'. Allowing just enough time for Corbet and his French escort to

Major Peirson – a portrait in the Jersey Museum

return to St Helier, Peirson led his fighting force into town where, at Charing Cross, he divided it into two columns for a pincer attack on the French who were mustered in the market place – now the Royal Square. In a short but bloody battle both leaders were to be mortally injured. Major Peirson, exposed bravely at the head of his column, was shot almost immediately. De Rullecourt, coming out of the Court House with the Lieutenant-Governor, was fired on and died six hours later. Within a quarter of an hour the French surrendered and the battle was won. Back at La Rocque the rearguard was also routed.

This last attempt by the French to gain Jersey had no glorious finale. The hero of the hour was dead and, at a court martial in London four months later, Major Moise Corbet was removed from office.

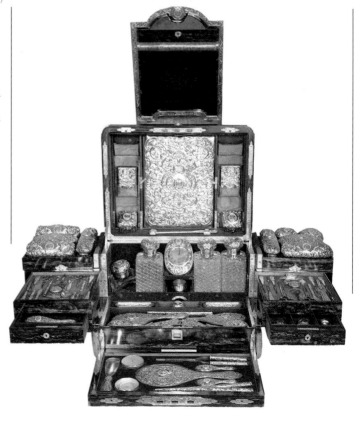

Jersey – West

Parishes of St Ouen, St Mary, St Peter and St Brelade

La Corbière

Map Ref: 85WV5448

The lighthouse on this south-west tip of the island was not built until the end of the last century, despite the fact that for hundreds of years, ships had come to grief on the surrounding rocks. It has even been said that the locals benefited too much from these disasters to put a stop to them. In the 15th century, for example, when a Spanish ship was wrecked, 'the sands of St Ouen's Bay were strewn with casks of wine'. Whatever the reason for the delay, following a decision in 1873 the first concrete lighthouse in the British Isles was constructed on a rock 500yd from the shore. It is now unmanned, and the electric light can be seen for 18 miles in good visibility. When needed, the foghorn sounds for five seconds in each minute.

It can be reached by foot at low tide, but visitors should take note of a warning on a memorial stone at the start of the causeway, and not

La Corbière Lighthouse.
Inset: the Jersey Radio Tower, Corbière

try to cross when the tide is coming in. The German observation tower to the east of the lighthouse now houses the ship-to-shore communications centre, and on the road to Petit Port there is a German bunker which is open to the public on Saturdays.

Several caves can be reached by a pathway next to the Highlands Hotel. The Smugglers' Cave is exceptionally deep and worth exploring at low tide.

La Grève de Lecq

Map Ref: 85WV5855

A popular beach, this, with its little stream, the stubby pier now rebuilt after being destroyed by a storm in 1885, and its coarse, yellow sand once used to purify the island's water. To the east is a 270ft mound known as Le Castel de Lecq. This is thought to have been used as a hill-fort during the Iron Age, and a refuge from invaders in medieval times. Evidence of much of its early history has been lost, through constant cultivation, the building of a military guard house in 1779 and the use of the mound by the

Germans in World War II.

The guard house was the first of several defences put up here to fend off a French invasion. In 1780 the tower in the centre of the bay was built. Later, a gun battery was installed in front of it and more guns placed on the hillside at each end of the bay. At the beginning of the 19th century, when the fear of a French invasion was at its height, a barracks was built to accommodate 150 men. This now belongs to the National Trust for Jersey, which has not only restored it, but also installed several displays to recreate life as it once was at this lonely outpost. One barrack room is laid out with beds and uniforms, while another has a display of military equipment and records. In a third room there is a display of old horse-drawn vehicles and the stables, harness room, ablution blocks and cells are also open to the public.

La Grève de Lecq is tucked up in the north-western corner of the parish of St Mary – one of the smallest parishes in Jersey, both in area and in population. There are narrow roads and old farmhouses, and many field names recall a history of sheep-breeding in the area, with knitting a major industry in the parish in the 16th and 17th centuries. The coast offers splendid scenery.

A peaceful scene on the coast at La Grève de Lecq belies its strategic importance in past times of conflict

Les Landes

Map Ref: 85WV5455

A windswept heathland at the north-westerly tip of the island, it not only has the finest views of the other main Channel Islands, but also some spectacular scenery of its own, as well as a mystery castle, a holy rock, a rifle range and a racecourse.

Gros Nez Castle was already a ruin by 1540, as is shown on a map of that date. The presence of a 'machicoulis' gallery for dropping stones on to the enemy below means that it could not have been built before the 14th century, and it was probably built then as a refuge from the constant French raids. It may well have been dismantled during the French occupation of 1461-68.

Nearby are relics of the 20th-century German Occupation – an observation tower, gun emplacements, bunkers and anti-aircraft mountings.

A short coastal walk to the south leads to an object of veneration and worship for thousands of years. Le Pinacle is a 200ft-high rock, set dramatically at the edge of a natural amphitheatre. Excavations have shown that people first came here around 4500BC when standing stones *(menhirs)* may have been worshipped. Le Pinacle continued as a ceremonial site until as late as

AD300 when a Gallo-Roman temple or *fanum* was built, possibly by those who wanted to keep to the old religion rather than adopt the worship of Roman gods. There is a tunnel cave running underneath Le Pinacle which can be waded through at low tide, always with great respect for swift tides and currents.

Race meetings are held at the Les Landes track eight or nine times a year, with the biggest fixture over August Bank Holiday.

Les Quennevais

Map Ref: 85WV5849

This is the island's second largest shopping centre, saving many people in the west the time and trouble of driving into St Helier. The name is derived from the Jersey-French word for hemp, *chènevière*, which was once cultivated here. However, the fertility of the area was destroyed on St Catherine's Day 1495 by a sandstorm. Until the sand dunes were stabilised by vegetation some 300 years ago, sandstorms were a recurring problem. In 1668 it is recorded that land in the area was 'swallowed up by the sand and abandoned by its owners'.

The Corbière Walk, on the track of the old railway, can be joined by steps down from the shopping precinct, and a comparatively new

attraction, the Lavender Farm, can be found just round the corner in Rue de Pont Marquet.

Noir Mont

Map Ref: 86WV6047

The 'Black Mountain', to give a literal translation, was bought after the last war by the States, the Island Parliament, as a permanent war memorial. It is certainly a fitting place, for while offering peace and solitude, it also has lasting evidence of the horror of war.

One of the three observation towers built by the German occupying force is situated here, as is Batterie Lothringen, one of four naval artillery batteries installed in the Channel Islands.

On certain Sundays and on Thursday evenings during the summer this massive installation is opened to the public by the Channel Islands Occupation Society who maintain it.

One of the many defensive towers built between 1810 and 1814 is situated at the southernmost tip of the point. La Tour de Vinde is now used as a shipping marker with an unattended flashing light.

There are plenty of paths on this headland, offering a variety of views, and it is also possible to climb down to the shoreline, good for crabbing.

on the weather for the flowers to grow, require a host of patient flower-making volunteers.

The parade used to finish with the 'battle' proper, when spectators tore the flowers off the floats and hurled them at each other. Some say that missiles other than flowers began to be thrown, but for whatever reason the custom stopped, which means the floats can be admired for several more days. The Battle of Flowers is now part of a week-long festival.

The Battle of Flowers Museum in St Ouen's Parish shows prize-winning entries constructed by Miss Florence Bechelet, who began competing in the event in 1934 and went on to win repeatedly with her figures made of hare's tail and marram grass.

Battle of Flowers, Guernsey

As in Jersey, Guernsey's Battle of Flowers, held as the climax to the North Show in Sausmarez Park on the fourth Thursday in August, is the most popular event of the year.

The floats take months to design, build and cover in flowers. Allotments, gardens and fields are sown with asters, marigolds, carnations and hydrangeas to produce the millions of blooms needed. Competitors in the various classes

Battle of Flowers

Jersey's greatest tourism event of the year is the Battle of Flowers, held on a Thursday afternoon at the beginning of August. Many visitors plan their holidays around this colourful cavalcade on Victoria Avenue, which now attracts crowds of around 60,000. The highlight of the whole parade is the spectacular floats decorated with literally thousands of flowers. They are joined by several marching bands, majorette troupes and celebrities. Miss Battle of Flowers, chosen in the preceding spring for her beauty and ability to represent the island, is joined in her special float by Mr Battle – a star of stage, screen or sport.

The Battle started in 1902 to celebrate the Coronation of King Edward VII, and was held at its present venue – a fitting tribute to the late Queen Victoria. So successful was this first event that it continued with the exception of the war years, until 1928. Then the venue changed to Springfield Stadium until World War II and the Occupation put an end to such festivities. In 1951 a group of local businessmen decided to revive the Battle as part of a tourism drive, and put it back on Victoria Avenue.

Miss Battle came into existence in 1953, and the following year

Anthony Steele was chosen as the first male star to accompany the Carnival Queen.

The floats have changed a great deal over the years, as the exhibitors have become more skilled in the arts of designing, constructing and decorating. At one time hydrangea blooms were entwined in wire mesh, but now the heads of varieties such as chrysanthemums, asters and carnations are glued on.

Come the week of the Battle, volunteers are to be found in packing sheds all over Jersey frantically snipping and sticking. Paper exhibits, while not dependent

Top: a colourful entry in the Battle of Flowers, Jersey, 1985
Bottom: a flashback to August 1905, and the Battle of Flowers as it used to be in Guernsey

spend most of the night before the battle decking the floats.

After the show floats appear all around the island, with collecting boxes for various charities under them, as they continue to enchant people until the flowers fade.

Portelet Bay (Le Portelet)

Map Ref: 86WV6046

This sheltered beach is reached by steps – quite a number of them – so is not recommended for anyone that has difficulty in walking. Those who do make it will appreciate its beauty, though a warning should be given that bathing can be dangerous around the natural bridge connecting L'Ile au Guerdain and the beach.

Many call this islet in the centre of the bay 'Janvrin's Tomb'. This relates to a sad incident in 1721 when a St Brelade man, one Philippe Janvrin, was captain of a ship *Esther*. Plague broke out on board just as he was about to bring the vessel into Jersey, and while it was anchored off-shore, he died. His body could not be brought ashore, so he was buried on L'Ile au Guerdain. His body was later removed to St Brelade. The round tower was built at the beginning of the 19th century.

St Aubin

Map Ref: 86WV6048

Although not big, St Aubin has always been Jersey's second town. Its quaint streets and old houses make it a charming place to explore. It was never the capital of the island, but during the 17th and 18th centuries it was more prosperous as a port than St Helier, and merchants built spacious houses with cellars to accommodate their goods close to the busy harbour. The Old Court House, which is one of the oldest and tallest of the buildings overlooking the harbour, is said to have been the venue for auctions by privateers, back from plundering foreign shipping.

Sheltered from south-westerly gales, St Aubin offers a safe harbour

Entrance to the lovely St Brelade's Parish Church

As there was no road linking St Aubin with St Helier until the 19th century, there was a market here from at least the 16th century. The National Westminster Bank is now in a reconstruction of the last St Aubin market, built in 1826.

The railway to St Helier was opened in 1870, and trains continued to run until 1936. The old Terminus Hotel is now St Brelade's Parish Hall, and the track to La Corbière is a popular walk.

Private boats fill the harbour and the Royal Channel Islands Yacht Club, of which Lillie Langtry was the first woman member, is alongside. St Aubin's Fort was improved by the British in 1840 and re-altered by the Germans during World War II. There have been defences on the site since 1542.

St Brelade's Bay

Map Ref: 85WV5848

The beach here is probably the most popular in the island, and certainly it is ideal for bathing and wind-surfing. The Winston Churchill Memorial Park, on the other side of the road is also worth a visit.

St Brelade's Parish Church nestles close to the sea, in what must be the most beautiful setting for any place of worship. Inside, the church is equally beautiful, with its

unrendered granite walls and classic Norman shape. The Fishermen's Chapel, which stands alongside, has recently been restored showing some fine 14th- and 15th-century murals including 'Man's Redemption' and 'The Last Judgment'. St Brelade's also has the shortest 'perquage' or sanctuary path in the island, along which fugitives were led to the sea after seeking sanctuary in the church.

The road leading between the church and the new cemetery takes us to Le Coleron, the site of a 19th-century defensive battery. Across the road is the tomb of Jesse Boot, 1st Baron Trent of Nottingham, the founder of Boots the Chemists, along with that of his wife and the second Baron.

The other end of the bay, Ouaisné, is far less crowded, and the open area behind the sea wall, La Commune de Bas, is a favourite habitat of the rare Dartford warbler. A path runs above the Smugglers' Inn to Portelet Common, a large heathland with spectacular views.

St Ouen's Bay

Map Ref: 85WV5651

This sandy bay stretches for almost the entire length of the west coast. Families with young children will prefer the southern end where the waves are more gentle, while surfers choose the centre, north of the El Tico restaurant, where the swell can be as good as anywhere in the world for this sport.

Sand racing, similar to grass track racing, is held here three or four times a year, and there is also much to interest the historian. Maison de Garde de St Pierre was re-built in 1765 and is now painted white as a navigation marker; La Rocco Tower (started in 1795) was built on rocks at the southern end of the bay and was badly damaged during the last war, but renovated after an appeal in 1969. There are two Martello towers, so-called because their design resembles a tower at Mortella Point in Corsica which successfully warded off attacking British warships. Of these, Kempt Tower, named after Sir James Kempt, one of Wellington's generals at Waterloo, is now an Interpretation Centre for the whole bay, including Les Mielles, the vast inland conservation area.

Standing displays, pictures and audio-visual presentations at the centre explain the importance of the area for its past and its wildlife. Talks are given, guides on several subjects are available and there are regular walks for those interested in birds, flowers and the German Occupation.

St Ouen's Manor (Le Manoir de St Ouen)

Map Ref: 85WV5853

The grounds of this ancient manor are open on Tuesday afternoons, offering a chance to see part of the ancestral seat of one of the oldest families in Jersey: the de Carterets, Seigneurs of St Ouen, who owned land here before 1066 and who are still in residence.

The oldest surviving part of the manor is the south tower, built in 1380, and over the centuries the de Carterets, who played a major role in the island's history, extended their home accordingly. The chapel, built around the same time as the south tower, was desecrated during the Civil War and again during World War II, when it was used by the Germans as a store-house and butcher's shop. Now re-dedicated, it has a fine pre-Reformation altar-stone with five crosses representing the wounds of Christ.

History is everywhere. Two brothers who gained positions at the court of Henry VIII made the far east field into a jousting ground, while near the upper pond lies a plaque commemorating a more recent event, the execution by firing squad in 1941 of a young Frenchman, François Scornet, who took the blame for an attempted escape from France in a small fishing boat.

The moat and granite walls of beautiful St Ouen's Manor – family seat of the de Carterets for nearly 850 years

St Peter's Valley

Map Ref: 86WV6051

The National Trust own land here where one can walk through wooded côtils (steep fields) from Tesson Mill to beyond Le Moulin de Quetivel. Le Moulin de Quetivel itself has been restored by the Trust and is open to the public. Start on the top floor, where there is an exhibition explaining the history of Jersey mills and the methods used, then work down to the ground, seeing how it all works.

Further up the valley is a more recent attraction, the Fantastic Tropical Gardens. These were originally laid out in the 1950s with many rare and exotic plants. In the new Fantastic Gardens, one can walk, eat and shop in several 'countries', each with its own theme and national costumes. There are surprises everywhere – children love it.

During World War II great tunnels were driven deep into the hillsides around the valley, including the German Military Underground Hospital – also open to the public.

AA recommends:
Beaumont:
Hotel: Hotel L'Hermitage, 2-star, *tel.* (0534) 33314
Corbière:
Restaurant: Sea Crest Hotel Restaurant, Petit Port, 3-fork, *tel.* (0534) 42687
L'Etacq:
Hotel: Lobster Pot Hotel and Restaurant, 3-star, *tel.* (0534) 82888
Campsite: Summer Lodge Campsite, Leoville, 3-pennant, *tel.* (0534) 81921

Five oriental themes are displayed in the Fantastic Tropical Gardens

St Aubin:
Restaurant: Old Court House Inn, St Aubin's Harbour, 2-fork, *tel.* (0534) 41156
Guesthouse: Panorama St Aubin, High St, *tel.* (0534) 42429
St Brelade:
Hotels: Atlantic, La Moye, St Brelade's Bay, 4-star, *tel.* (0534) 44101
Hotel l'Horizon, St Brelade's Bay, 4-star, *tel.* (0534) 43101
Château Valeuse, Rue de Valeuse, St Brelade's Bay, 3-star, *tel.* (0534) 43476
Beau Rivage, 2-star, *tel.* (0534) 45983
Campsite: Rose Farm, Route des Genets, 3-pennant, *tel.* (0534) 41231

Jersey – Central

Parishes of St John, St Lawrence, Trinity and St Helier

Bonne Nuit

Map Ref: 86WV6455

Smuggling was rife around this secluded harbour until 1736, when the army moved in. The military presence was small at first, just a guard house, a cannon boulevard and a powder magazine, but enough to deter all but the most wily entrepreneur. Now it is pedestrians who can most enjoy the surroundings. To the east of the bay are two cliff paths, so a circular walk is possible. This goes by La Crête Fort, built in 1835 and now a country retreat for the island's Lieutenant-Governor, and then past the Cheval Roc Hotel, built on the site of a military barracks. From the top one can look down on Le Cheval Guillaume, the rock in the middle of the bay. At one time, on midsummer's day, people from all over the island used to come to Bonne Nuit to be rowed around this rock to avoid bad luck.

The view from La Tête de Frémont, to the west of the bay, is well worth the steep climb, and for those who prefer just to be sheltered by the 400ft cliffs, the bathing is good at high tide. However romantic the claim, the name of this bay has nothing to do with Charles II escaping to France from here saying 'Bonne Nuit Belle Jersey'. It is much older, and in the 12th century a chapel called de Bono Nocte existed here.

Bouley Bay

Map Ref: 87WV6754

Although there are similarities between this bay and neighbouring Bonne Nuit, such as the fortifications and the surrounding high cliffs, there is one important difference. Here the shingle beach shelves steeply, so although the bay is excellent for skin-divers, it is dangerous for children and inexperienced swimmers. The water is so deep that in the 19th century it was proposed to build a large harbour here. This never materialised, probably because the land access is so difficult.

The windy road leading from the top of the 500ft cliff to the bay is most famous for the hill climbs. These have been organised since the 1930s by the Jersey Motor Cycle and Light Car Club which now holds club events on the Easter and Spring Bank Holiday Mondays, and a round of the British Hill Climb Championship in July. Anyone driving up the road will appreciate the skill in manoeuvring a vehicle from bottom to top in 39 seconds.

There are several walks in the area. As well as the cliff path, it is possible to climb from the beach to Le Jardin d'Olivet, to the east. This was the field of a 16th-century battle in which an invading French expedition was routed and a Jersey lieutenant-bailiff killed.

Like Bonne Nuit, this little harbour was used by smugglers, who may have started the legend of the Black Dog of Bouley, as big as a man and with eyes like saucers, said to roam the cliff-tops on dark nights.

Four-hundred-foot cliffs protect the beaches of Bonne Nuit Bay and offer breathtaking views from the top

The slipway at Bouley Bay, one of the best places in Jersey to see volcanic rock. The multi-coloured pebbles date back millions of years

Inset: a 1011yd breakneck climb for motorcycles, karts, cars and cycles

Eric Young Orchid Foundation

Map Ref: 87WV6652

At any time of the year, flower-lovers will find much to admire in this purpose-built centre opened in 1986.

It is named after the late Eric Young, well-known in Jersey as a philanthropist and throughout the world as an orchid expert. During his lifetime, he had worked towards setting up this foundation. His first glasshouses in Jersey were in St Helier, where he built up one of the finest private collections in Europe. During the 1970s he became recognised world-wide for his work in breeding new hybrids, all bearing Jersey place-names.

In 1976 work began towards setting up a charitable trust to continue this work, and in 1981 this site was found. In the complex there are five growing houses, where a computer controls the heating, shading, ventilation and humidity to suit the different species. There is also an incredibly beautiful display area where visitors can enjoy, at close range, the colour and splendour of these exotic plants.

The foundation continues Eric Young's work, creating new hybrids and winning recognition and awards throughout the world, and in its first year alone it also provided blooms for the wedding of the Duke and Duchess of York, the Chelsea Flower Show and an exhibition in Harrods.

Fine displays from the Eric Young Orchid Foundation

colony who are not yet old enough to venture into the half-acre playpark.

Other species here are orang-utans, spectacled bears, lemurs and tamarins; there are iguanas in the Gaherty Reptile House, and birds range from pink Chilean flamingoes at the lakeside to the tiny Rodrigues Fody.

The grounds are a marvellous setting for a picnic, or one can eat at the Dodo Café.

Millbrook

Map Ref: 86WV6250

The Coronation Park is particularly popular with children, while St Matthew's Church is the only one decorated throughout by Lalique.

Both these places exist because of the benefaction of the widow of Baron Trent, the founder of Boots the Chemists shops. Florence, Lady Trent, lived at Villa Millbrook, the other side of St Aubin's Road. After laying out the park, she gave it to the island in 1937 as a resting place for the aged and a recreational area for the young. There is now a playpark, a paddling pool and a venture playground for the disabled as well as beautifully kept gardens.

The interior of St Matthew's Glass Church at Millbrook

Top: flamingoes on the pond at Jersey Zoo

Jersey Wildlife Preservation Trust

Map Ref: 87WV6753

Allow plenty of time to enjoy this most special zoo. The Trust is different from other zoos not only because it was founded by world-famous author and naturalist Gerald Durrell, but also, as its name implies, because it is not really a zoo at all, but a breeding centre for endangered species.

Breeding colonies of animals, reptiles and birds that might otherwise have become extinct have been established here with, for some, the ultimate aim of one day

Inset, bottom: Jersey Zoo – the Jersey Wildlife Preservation Trust – offers possibly the world's rarest collection of animals. Here are the golden tamarind lion and one of the zoo's successes – lowland gorillas

returning them into the wild.

None of this need deter those who want just to see these rare creatures. The cleverly designed cages and runs not only benefit the inmates, but also increase the visitors' enjoyment. One of Jersey's great successes is the lowland gorilla. In a fine modern complex, Jambo, the most prolific captive male gorilla in the world, reigns supreme along with his wives and their offspring. There is even a short-circuit television screen, so that visitors can view the tiniest members of the

A few years before she donated the park, Florence Lady Trent renovated the simple Chapel-of-ease at Millbrook as a memorial to her husband. The brilliant French glassworker, René Lalique, was engaged and everything, including the altar-rail, the 12ft-high cross, the pillars, windows and font, are all made out of his beautiful, slightly opaque glass. There are four glass angels behind the altar in the Lady Chapel and two more by the door. St Matthew's is known locally as 'The Glass Church'.

Differences

Many people choose the Channel Islands as a holiday destination because of their similarity to the UK. In the main, islanders speak English, eat the same food, have familiar multiple stores and deal in pounds and pence. But the discerning visitor will find differences equally attractive.

It is true that English is universally spoken but French is still used for legal documents and in the prayers said before States and court sittings. Most important of all, many islanders still speak the local Norman-French – a language similar to that spoken by country folk in Normandy. This really came into its own during the Occupation, as it is well nigh impossible for foreigners to understand, and it is used still, especially at country events such as cattle shows.

Place names are usually French or are derived from the names of past owners. Hence in Jersey *Les Mouriers,* meaning mulberries, *La Brugère* meaning heather heath and *Les Noyers* meaning walnut trees, while Morel Farm, La Billotterie and La Maitrerie at one time belonged respectively to the families Morel, Billot and Le Maistre.

In Guernsey there are several places called *marais* (marsh) and *les Landes* (common). *Hougue* means 'hill' while a *douit* is a brook.

Before the Reformation all Jersey's parish churches had *perquage* or sanctuary paths, running to the sea. Those who took sanctuary in the church were escorted down the perquage path to the sea if they swore to leave the island forever. Some paths survive: the one from St. Brelade is the shortest, while that from St Martin's Parish Church makes a pleasant walk to St Catherine's Bay.

Lanes leading to parish churches in Guernsey are marked by stones bearing crosses, as at the Bailiff's Cross in St Andrew's. Here pall-bearers could 'change shoulders' without the Devil leaping into the box with the deceased.

Only the *Seigneur* could have a *colombier,* or dovecote. The pigeons were a kind of tax on farmers, converting their crops into meat for the Seigneur. In Jersey there are 11 *colombiers* in existence. One, belonging to the National Trust, is in the grounds of Longueville Manor (Le Manoir de Longueville) Hotel, and one is at Samarès Manor (Le Manoir de Samarés), which is open to the public.

In Sark the Seigneur still holds this privilege, but keeps only a few white fan-tailed doves.

Roads have specific island features. Sark's roads have no metalled surface, making them dusty, while Herm has only footpaths. Guernsey's military roads, built in the early 19th century to allow troops easy access to likely sites of invasion, are identified by pavements. These

A 'lavoir' on La Marquanderie Hill, St Brelade

allowed people room to get out of the way of the marching militia men, but are now used as passing points by wide vehicles.

Two things to look out for at the roadside in Jersey are *lavoirs* and *abreuvoirs.* The first are places for washing linen and the second for watering animals. These are usually built on the course of a stream.

Fiefs or manors had their own courts. A fief court building can be seen at Sausmarez Manor, but most met at open air sites with a large stone seat for court officials. The court of Fief Jean de Gaillard can be seen just outside the south gate of St Saviour's churchyard.

Strong, if friendly, rivalry still exists between the islands. In Guernsey the old nickname for Jerseyman is a *crapaud* (toad), because the toad is found in Jersey but not in Guernsey. In Jersey the people of Guernsey are known as 'donkeys'.

Sion

Map Ref: 86WV6452

At first glance, it would seem this tiny village is totally dominated by its Methodist church, built in 1881 in the style of a classical temple. Just to the north of the church, in the garden of 'Centre House' is the stone marking the centre of the

island, and just across the main road is an interesting cemetery called Macpéla. Here are buried some of the European exiles who flocked to Jersey in the mid-19th century. Each funeral was used by the colony as a political stand. They would march to the cemetery

Milking time at Heatherbrae Farm

behind the red flag, and at the burial, inflammatory speeches were made – often by that most famous French exile, Victor Hugo.

A few hundred yards up the main road, on the right, is Heatherbrae Farm. This is open to the public, who can learn about milk production and enjoy at close quarters the sight of the pretty Jersey cow.

AA recommends:
Rozel Bay:
Hotel: Chateau La Chaire, Rozel Valley, 2-star, Country House, *tel.* (0534) 63354

St John:
Garage: Seaton, Windsor Villa, Route du Mont, Mado, *tel.* (0534) 61389

St Lawrence:
Hotel: Little Grove, Rue de Haut, 3-star, *tel.* (0534) 25321

Trinity:
Guesthouse: Highfield Country Hotel, Route du Ebenezer, *tel.* (0534) 62194

Jersey – East
Parishes of St Martin, St Saviour, Grouville and St Clement
Gorey (Gouray)

Map Ref: 87WV7050

The best known and most photographed part of this small fishing village is the pier, its row of houses dwarfed by Mont Orgueil Castle towering above them. The castle is Jersey's oldest, repelling French attacks from the 13th century onwards, but the pier was not built until 1820, and the houses were built on land reclaimed during its construction. There had been a harbour here before, but it was in no way big enough to cope with the massive growth in the oyster industry at the beginning of the 19th century when the English fishing companies moved in. The whole village grew up around this time and by 1832 there were around 2000 men employed in the oyster trade. It was then that Gouray Church was built, and several smaller churches of other denominations were also built in the main street. The companies' greed caused overdredging, and by the middle of the century the industry had largely died out.

This is the only official sea port in the island, apart from St Helier. It has its own customs house to cope with the regular ferries which ply to and from the nearby Normandy coast. The promenade, overlooking the picturesque harbour, is bordered by gardens laid out on the original 1891 Eastern Railway track. A fountain in the shape of a skeletal boat is set in the

Top: Mont Orgueil Castle towers above the harbour

middle of these gardens. It commemorates another of the port's industries, that of shipbuilding, and along its keel are engraved the names of the ships that came out of the local yards.

AA recommends:
Gorey:
Hotel: Old Court House, 3-star, *tel.* (0534) 54444
Restaurant: Galley, 1-fork, *tel.* (0534) 53456
Guesthouse: Royal Bay Hotel, *tel.* (0534) 53318

Green Island (La Motte)

Map Ref: 87WV6746

Bathing, rock-fishing and exploration are all recommended from this sandy beach, which has the distinction of being the most southerly point in the British Isles.

Bottom: the ferry from the port to Carteret, France

The island itself is about 300 yards from the shore and can easily be reached at low tide, when the sea recedes some two miles along this coastline, offering a moon-like landscape and a good opportunity for low-water fishing. Be careful, however, not to be among those who have to be rescued by the Fire Service: when the tide does turn, the sea races through the gulleys at a tremendous pace and can catch out even the most experienced adult, to say nothing of a child caught up in the delights of rock-pools and shrimp-nets.

Some 1¼ miles out to sea lies Ic-Ho Tower, built as part of the island's defences in 1810. Green Island itself, properly called La Motte, was, until comparatively recently, joined to the mainland. In 1911 a Neolithic cemetery was discovered on its summit. Some of the rectangular graves can now be seen at the Hougue Bie Museum.

Royal Bay of Grouville

Map Ref: 87WV7048

This long strand running between Mont Orgeuil and the village of La Rocque is ideal for swimming and wind-surfing. It is also possible to walk the length of the sea-wall, though beware the golfer as the Royal Jersey Golf Club is situated on the common beyond.

Golfing on the Royal Jersey course on Grouville Common

To give its official title, this is the Royal Bay of Grouville, a name given because of Queen Victoria's state visit in 1859. At that time there was much more gritty sand on the beach, but during the last war over a million tons of it were removed from both the beach and the common, to be used to make concrete, an act which caused untold damage.

There are reminders, too, of earlier troubles. Fort William, now an unusual private house, was built in 1760, swiftly followed by Fort Henry, which is used by the Golf Club, and there are five more defensive towers still in existence.

This is a birdwatchers' paradise. Wading birds such as curlew, oystercatcher, redshank, plover and dunlin feed here during the winter months, while the common and sandwich tern keep company with the oystercatcher during the summer. The grey heron uses the larger off-shore reefs as a winter roost and from November until April brent geese are a common sight.

La Rocque has been a fishing village since the Middle Ages and there are still men in the village who make their living from the sea. It is a constant fascination to watch them wending their way through the jagged rocks that surround this natural harbour. No wonder de Rullecourt, when he invaded the island on the eve of the Battle of Jersey, needed a local pilot to guide him.

La Hougue Bie

Map Ref: 87WV6850

Legends and tales of the supernatural surround this 40ft mound, built in Neolithic times to cover a passage grave and now administered by La Société Jersiaise. The word Hougue comes from the Norse *haugre* meaning a burial mound, while 'Bie' is thought to have derived from the Norman family Hambye who, it is said, owned the site. One legend has it that one of the chapels on the summit, dedicated to Our Lady of the Dawn, was built in the 12th century by a daughter of the house of Hambye who had been banished to Jersey. Each day at dawn she is said to have stood there looking at the coast of France, trying to see her forbidden lover. One morning she had a vision of the Virgin Mary, and so she built a chapel.

The grave below is still intact and can be entered. It is 50ft long and

La Hougue Bie – an ancient sacred site

dates from about 3000BC. The great stones used to form the grave were dragged from quarries as far away as Bouley Bay and St Helier, and the mound is made from earth, rubble and limpet shells.

There are two chapels on top of the mound. The later one was built in 1520 after the owner, Dean Mabon, had visited the Holy Land. He called it the Jerusalem Chapel, and in the hope of attracting pilgrims to the site, also built a replica of the Holy Sepulchre beneath it.

There are several museums within the grounds. Relics of the Occupation can be seen in a concrete bunker built originally by the Germans during the last war as a communications centre. Also here are a railway exhibition, an archaeological room and an excellent agricultural museum showing aspects of farming through the ages.

Mont Orgueil Castle

Map Ref: 87WV7150

This must surely be one of the most beautiful of all Britain's ancient castles. Translated, the name means Mount Pride. Although there are known to have been fortifications on the site since early times the present castle dates back to the reign of King John. When he lost Normandy in 1204, France became enemy territory, and a fort on this hill, just ten miles from the Normandy coast, was a necessity. The castle was strengthened and enlarged over the years, and apart from a sorry period in the 15th century when the island was invaded and occupied by the French for seven years, it normally withstood the constant raids.

In the late 16th century, the range of cannon-fire had increased to such an extent that it was thought the castle was redundant, and plans were drawn up for a new castle in the bay of St Helier. Fortunately that most famous of Jersey governors, Sir Walter Raleigh, insisted that Mont Orgueil was not pulled down.

The castle played an important part in the Civil War. It was held in the name of the King by Anne Dowse (whose husband was the governor Sir Philippe de Carteret),

Mont Orgueil Castle

until, following the Battle of Worcester in 1651, it was handed over to Commonwealth troops. During those troubled years prisoners from both sides were incarcerated in the dungeons.

During the French Revolution, many of France's fleeing nobility were entertained here by Admiral Philippe d'Auvergne who operated a pro-Royalist secret service from within its walls.

Exhibitions and tableaux at the castle depict its rich history, and an outdoor production of a Shakespeare play has become an annual event in August.

Rozel

Map Ref: 87WV6954

Visitors love this little village, with its gift shops, restaurants, sheltered beach and pretty harbour, built in 1829 when the oyster trade was at its peak.

At the beginning of this century, though, the village consisted only of a few fishermen's cottages and the barracks, erected in 1809 and now part of Le Couperon Hotel.

Rozel Valley, reached by the road running between the Rozel Bay Hotel and Château La Chaire, makes a pleasant walk. A 19-century botanist, Samuel William Curtis, lived here, and many trees and shrubs planted by him and his daughter still survive. Islanders make a point of coming here in early spring to see the giant Himalaya pink tulip tree in bloom, while in May, the nearby handkerchief tree attracts attention. A walk up the valley leads to Rozel Mill, one of Jersey's ancient windmills and now a private house.

Rozel, Jersey. Inset: Rozel Woods sanctuary path

St Catherine's Bay

Map Ref: 87WV7152

The 2300ft-long breakwater was
built in the mid-19th century as
part of Britain's defences against
France. It had been hoped to form
a harbour of refuge here, despite
strong recommendations that there
would never be a sufficient depth of
water to make it work. The task
was abandoned in 1849, but not
before the British government had
spent more than a quarter of a
million pounds of taxpayers' money
on the project. In 1876 ownership
of the breakwater was transferred to
the States of Jersey and now it is
used only by anglers and
pedestrians.

Three 18th-century defensive
towers can be seen around the bay
and, tunnelled into the rockface
opposite the breakwater, a World
War II gun emplacement is used to
keep fish commercially.

Samarès Manor
(Le Manoir de Samarès)

Map Ref: 87WV6747

Farm walks, herb talks and guided
tours of a stately home are three of
the many attractions on offer here.

All that remains of the original
Norman building is the crypt of the
chapel, but the *colombier* (dovecote)
is thought to be the oldest in the
island.

The gardens were laid out shortly
after the Civil War, but really came
into their own after 1924 when the
manor was bought by a shipping
magnate, Sir James Knott. With the
help of landscape designer Edward
White, he created gardens reputed

The beautiful gardens of Samarès Manor, St Clement

to be amongst the most beautiful in
Britain. These can still be enjoyed,
along with the more recent
innovation of an enormous herb
garden.

The manor's fascinating history is
well illustrated by an exhibition in
the morning room, and it is all the
more interesting because this is still
a home and a working farm. Entry
tickets are valid for a week, to allow
visitors to do justice to all that can
be seen.

AA recommends:
Archirondel:
Hotel: Les Arches, Archirondel Bay,
2-star, *tel.* (0534) 53839

St Clement:
Guesthouse: Belle Plage Hotel, Green
Island, *tel.* (0534) 53750

*The south side of Samarès Manor,
justly famous for its herb gardens*

St Clement's Bay:
Hotel: Hotel Ambassadeur, Greve
d''Azette, 3-star, *tel.* (0534) 24455
Restaurant: Shakespeare Hotel, Samarès
Coast Road, 3-fork, *tel.* (0534) 51915

St Martin:
Guesthouse: Le Relais de St Martin, *tel.*
(0534) 53271
Campsite: Rozel Camping Park,
Summerville Farm, 3-pennant, *tel.* (0534)
51989

St Saviour:
Hotel: Longueville Manor (off St
Helier/Grouville Rd A3), 4-red star,
1-rosette, Country House, *tel.* (0534)
25501
Garage: La Motte, Rue des Pres, *tel.*
(0534) 73777

A doorway in St Peter Port, typical of doorways in Guernsey with the double arch of stones over the top

Guernsey

St Peter Port

Map Ref: 89WV3378

St Peter Port is the capital town of Guernsey, home of the island's government, main harbour, finance centre and a considerable amount of housing. The town is in three parts, the oldest clustered around the parish church, high street and the waterfront which dates to mediaeval times and faces the harbour. The second part, sometimes called St Peter Port's 'new town', is on higher ground above the mediaeval area and features many excellent Georgian and Regency houses, while modern housing estates on the perimeter of the parish form the third part. These include the colloquially named 'millionaires' estates' in the Village de Putron and

A view overlooking the town of St Peter Port from the citadel on top of Castle Cornet

the old garrison quarters of Fort George – homes of some tax exiles.

The shopping centre of St Peter Port is one of the most attractive in Britain. The main areas have been designated pedestrian precincts and shoppers wander through the winding, cobbled streets, between buildings which have altered little in hundreds of years. Particularly distinctive and attractive are the streets with flights of steps.

Town, as local people call St Peter Port, is also home to some of the finest restaurants which, although they span a wide price range, offer superb value for money. Understandably, many specialise in sea food, particularly crabs, lobsters and flatfish.

Guernsey's seat of government is in the Royal Court House where the States of Deliberation, the island's parliament, meet each month. The building also houses the Magistrates Court and Royal Court, the equivalent of County, Crown and High Courts in England and Wales.

St Peter Port, whether watching the boats, or exploring the narrow

alleys and steps, is a place in which to unwind.

Aquarium and bathing places

Material needed to build the harbour piers and jetties was excavated from the base of cliffs at Les Terres and La Valette on the southern outskirts of St Peter Port. A sedate promenade to La Valette, ending in the bathing places and a tunnel which went to the more secluded beach of Soldier's Bay, was constructed.

Germans fortified the tunnel during the Occupation and after the war it was converted into a home for a commercial aquarium containing colourful tropical marine and freshwater fish, and local specimens. A number of tanks house mullet and bass shoals, plaice, turbot and brill hug the sandy bottom, while above them swims a portbeagle shark.

The bathing pools have an unusual cleaning mechanism – they are flooded by the sea twice a day! They were the only public swimming pools before Beau Sejour was built and are still immensely popular.

Guernsey Parish Map

St Peter Port Museum – built on the site of a concert pavilion

Beau Sejour

Many visitors wonder how Guernsey's population of just 55,000 people can support such an enterprise as this – the island's leisure centre. But since Beau Sejour opened in 1976, more than five million people have used the centre's sports hall, theatre, swimming pool, bars, health suite and exhibition facilities. They have

The museum tearoom has been converted from the bandstand of the old pavilion

watched top films, listened to pop concerts, heard hot gospel preachers, and hopped to the latest disco beat. Outside there are bowling greens and tennis courts, an inflated castle and astroglide on which youngsters bounce and slide, a climbing tower and BMX cycle track.

Although built with local people in mind, Beau Sejour also has a more serious side. Guernsey's climate is not always hot and sunny and the centre is designed to provide facilities during any wet parts of a holiday.

It has conference facilities for 2000 delegates with a 'sit down' dining capacity of 600 covers. The centre is home to a number of trade shows, including the Channel Islands' Boat Show and the Ideal Home Exhibition. Top pop artists and entertainers appear in concerts, mostly during the summer season.

Guernsey Museum and Art Gallery

Housed in beautiful gardens at Candie, overlooking the town, Herm and Sark, the building won the New Museum of the Year award in 1979 and tells the story of Guernsey and its people. A recent addition has provided an education wing for the museum and a headquarters for La Société Guernèsiaise, the local research society.

The society has added many exhibits in the museum to the collections of Frederick Lukis and Wilfred Carey, which were the first artefacts owned by the island. Lukis was an archaeologist who opened several ancient long tombs and dolmens in the early part of last century and Carey's collections of pictures, prints and ceramics were bequeathed to the museum in 1929.

The museum is based on a series of eight-sided rooms which link the main display areas, art gallery, shop, small theatre and coffee bar. The

St Peter Port Marina

An ornate old-fashioned sign tempts shoppers to fine wares

ginko tree and a greenhouse – reputedly the oldest in Guernsey.

Harbours and marinas

All sea-borne visitors and much of the containerised freight arrives at the harbour and passenger terminal. The port is home to a fishing fleet of about 20 boats. Day trips to Herm, Sark, Alderney and Jersey leave from the port, and a ferry service connects Fermain Bay, two miles down the coast. Three marinas cater for vast numbers of yachts, visitors from all over the world making them the modern equivalent of the Tower of Babel.

The first harbour to be built is now the Victoria Marina, in the centre of the complex. A sill was put across the mouth of the marina to ensure that the moored yachts are afloat, even on the lowest tide. The modern pool of St Peter Port was constructed when a pier connecting the South Esplanade to

Sheltered St Peter Port Harbour, a haven for seafarers for centuries

story of Guernsey is told by a series of displays starting with the geology, climate and natural history, continuing with man's influence on the island from Neolithic times.

Displays in the art gallery are changed frequently, and include temporary exhibitions of local artists' work, and celebrations of anniveraries of people, organisations and events.

The gardens offer camellias, fuschias and mimosa flower in season. In the lower garden is a wall-trained lemon which fruits out-of-doors, a fine specimen of the rare

Victor Hugo

Victor Marie Hugo (1802-1885) took a cold bath on the roof of his house in Hauteville, St Peter Port, at six every morning, and afterwards would stand gazing across the street at the house in which his mistress, Juliette Drouet, lived.

Hugo chose his house in Guernsey for the view across to 'my beloved France', from where he was exiled because of his political activities. He had been an enthusiast for Napoleon before switching his political loyalty in 1848 and becoming a republican representative in the popular assembly. Opposing the right-wing policies of Prince Louis-Napoleon and the establishment of the Second Empire, he fled from France in 1851 and spent much of the next 18 years in Guernsey. He found the cliff walks inspiring, and settled reasonably happily, writing two love-letters to Juliette each day, as well as some of his best work. *The Toilers of the Sea* was inspired by the island's fishing community and dedicated to the sailors of Guernsey. *Les Miserables* was also written while he was confined here.

Hauteville House was bought with the proceeds from a book of poems written just after his arrival. It soon became one of the most extraordinary properties in the Channel Islands, thanks to Hugo's DIY work, carving up furniture – which would now be greatly valued antiques – in order to make the cabinets, cupboards and furniture which fill the house today. It is open to the public and a guided tour lasts about an hour, winding up to the top of the four-storey building, where one can see the country for which Hugo longed. The house is owned by the City of Paris, and many of the visitors are French.

Hugo began his prolific writing career as a child: by 14 he had completed a tragedy, and by 20 he had won prizes for his poetry. He is considered by many to be France's greatest lyric poet, experimenting with language and rhythm and always sensitive to the sound and colour of words. *Les Feuilles d'Automne* and *Contemplations* describe the moods and emotions of the poet in rich, sonorous verse. In English the best known of his works include *The Hunchback of Notre Dame* and *Les Miserables*. His novels, always long, showed a concern and humanitarian interest in the problems and suffering of the common man. Some of his plays were sources for operatic librettos. *Hernani* and *Le Roi S'amuse* were set to music by Verdi, the latter becoming *Rigoletto*, while *Angelo* became Ponchielli's *La Gioconda*.

Hugo returned to France in 1870 and afterwards returned to Guernsey only on three short visits. Juliette died in 1883 and he followed her two years later, earning a state funeral in Paris.

The look-out from Victor Hugo's house

Castle Cornet was built in 1853. The Albert Marina was built between the Castle Emplacement and the south wall of the Victoria Marina. At the northern end of the harbour another huge jetty was built ending the White Rock. This pier supports the shipping terminal and docks on one side, while on the other is the North Marina.

Markets

These were built to house butchers whose activities around the Town Church attracted packs of vermin and created smells to which the congregation objected. They were strategically placed between the commercial part of St Peter Port, on the harbour front, and the new town overlooking it from the hilltop behind.

The French Halles, opposite the market, were built in 1782, but were found too small. The architect John Wilson, who designed many of the town's most interesting buildings, was called in to sort things out. Les Arcades were opened in 1830, to be followed by the Fish Market, with its superb roof, and Lower Vegetable Market by the end of the century. The smell of each market is left behind as the next is entered. The buildings are designed so that the natural draughts take smells up and away.

Traditionally dressed stall holders set up the colourful Old Guernsey Market outside the building in Market Square every Thursday afternoon from 2pm through the summer.

The Arcade, and fresh produce at St Peter Port Fish Market

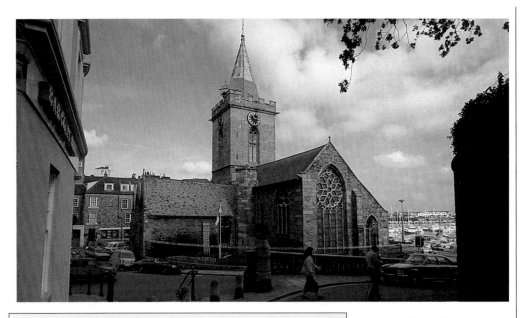

Castle Cornet

Castle Cornet links the year 1206 with the German Occupation in World War II: the strategic importance of the site has not diminished in almost 800 years. Built to protect the ships which ran from the south coast of England between Guernsey and Herm to Bordeaux and Bayonne, it also defended St Peter Port.

To the visitor it has more to offer than historical interest. Castle Cornet commands superb views, not only of St Peter Port and the pier connecting the castle to it, but also of the other Channel Islands and nearby parts of the French coast. Many people use the castle to keep watch over the modern vessels which ply their trade with the island.

There are museums to visit within the castle, including collections of arms, uniforms and a history of 201 RAF Squadron. But the best way to see Castle Cornet is by imagining that you are part of an invading force sacking the citadel.

The entrance is through a doorway tucked in the bastion – facing seawards to protect visitors from St Peter Port's gunfire! As you pass under a portcullis into the outer ward, the entrance is overlooked by the black cannon of the saluting battery which face out into the harbour. The area is connected to the barbican by a flight of steps which run up through a curtain wall – a relic of the French occupation in about 1338.

At this point, a diversion to the left leads to the Royal Battery, where, from April to October, at noon each day a cannon is fired on the order of a man in uniform who studies the Town Church clock through a telescope. The colourful ceremony is a re-enactment of the curfew gun fired to order Guernsey's garrison back to

barracks in Fort George, above St Peter Port.

Back on the route of an invading force, the barbican's entrance is marked by a portcullis protecting the castle's second line of defence – a pit and drawbridge. Although neither remain, a recess housing the mechanism can still be seen.

The prisoners' walk, named because convicts were exercised there when the castle was the gaol, leads under another 13th-century portcullis to the site of the tower. Used as a gunpowder store, it was struck by lightning in 1672 and blew up, killing the wife and mother of the Governor of Guernsey, Lord Hatton. Guernsey's governors have lived elsewhere on the island since.

A set of steps leads up to a citadel on the top of the rocky islet, where evidence of the German Occupation can be seen. Range finders mark the distance to nearby Alderney, Herm and Sark, and machine gun bullets from a British air raid have scarred the concrete fortifications. Outer ramparts which skirt the castle can be explored on the way down from the top.

The prison tower of Castle Cornet

The beautiful Town Church – often referred to as St Peter Port Cathedral

The Royal Court House

An unlikely place to visit but certainly worth the trip. Once a month, usually for two days, the island's government meet in the building. There are Magistrates, Juvenile, Petty Debts, Civil or Royal Court sittings daily.

The building also houses the offices of the Greffe, or record room, and the Bailiff's offices. A maximum of three courts can sit at one time – they are limited by the number of rooms available. The Royal Court, which corresponds to the County, Crown and High Courts of England and Wales, sits in the room which is also used for States of Deliberation meetings. Civil cases are heard in La Cour Ordinaire by the ordinary division of the Royal Court. Petty debt, juvenile and criminal cases are in the third room – the Magistrates Court – along with land conveyancing registrations.

The Bailiff, or the deputy, presides over the Royal Court and the States meetings, while HM Greffier is clerk of the court. The island has a fixed jury of 12 jurats, who can also act as magistrates. They are elected by the States of Election – the island's parliament – together with rectors and parish representatives.

St James Concert and Assembly Hall

One of the many buildings designed by architect John Wilson, it was built to commemorate the victory of the Battle of Waterloo in 1815 and was consecrated in 1818. The church became the site of a dispute 155 years later when plans to demolish it and turn the area into a car park were opposed by a group

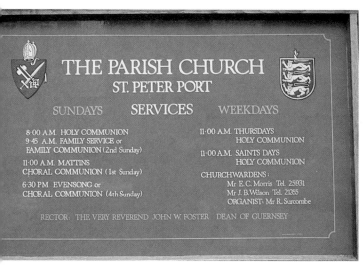

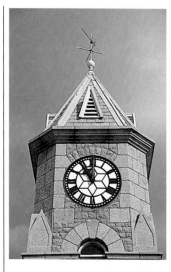

Above: services at St Peter Port Town Church
Above right: the Weighbridge Clock

of people who called themselves the Friends of St James. Eventually they won and almost half a million pounds was spent restoring the building by the island's government.

It was tastefully converted into a concert and assembly hall which is run by the Friends. The acoustics in the 600-seat building are superb and it has become the cultural centre of the island with a range of concerts, recitals, exhibitions and even tea dances. Details of coming events are published by the Friends of St James in a leaflet.

Town Church

The Anglican religious centre of the island started life as one of a series of fishermen's small churches. It has also served as a refuge against attack and housed the parish fire pump in its north aisle for many years.

The main entrance is in Church Square, and the nave is reached by walking past two rows of pews. The altar faces the west door, with a rounded Norman arch, and in the middle of the aisle the thick walls of the original church can be seen.

The south transept was added in 1466, its slender, more delicate pillars contrasting with the heavy Norman piers elsewhere in the church. The life of St Peter, to whom it is dedicated, is depicted in scenes carved on the choir stalls in the chancel.

Elizabeth College, close to Candie Gardens and the Museum, dominates the skyline of St Peter Port

Many of the monuments and tombs inside the Town Church reflect the lives of Guernsey's greatest men. These include privateer Captain Nicholas Le Messurier, who was killed on the high seas in 1759, and General Sir Isaac Brock who led the successful British troops at the Battle of Queenston Heights, in 1812.

AA recommends:
St Peter Port:
Hotels: Old Government House, Ann's Pl, 4-star, *tel.* (0481) 24921
St Pierre Park, Rohais, 4-star, *tel.* (0481) 28282
La Collinette, St Jacques, 3-star, *tel.* (0481) 710331
Le Frégate, Les Côtils, 3-star, *tel.* (0481) 24624
Hotel de Havelet, Havelet, 2-star, *tel.* (0481) 22199
Moore's, Pollet, 2-star, *tel.* (0481) 24452
Restaurants: Le Nautique, Quay Steps, 3-fork, *tel.* (0481) 21714
Nino's Ristorante Italiano, Lefevre St, 1-fork, *tel.* (0481) 23052
Self Catering: La Collinette Hotel Self Catering Cottages, St Jacques, *tel.* (0481) 710331
Guesthouses: Midhurst House, Candie Rd, *tel.* (0481) 24391
Changi Lodge Hotel, Les Baissieres, *tel.* (0481) 56446
Garage: Vale, Braye Rd, Vale, *tel.* (0481) 46381

Right: Town Church door
Above right: Choir stall

Guernsey – North
Parishes of Vale and St Sampson
L'Ancresse Common

Map Ref: 89WV3483

This huge recreational area has a golf course, several beaches, an occasional racecourse, and a firing range. An area is set aside for aero modellers to fly their planes at Chouet, and there are a number of archaeological sites. L'Ancresse is common land – golfers have to avoid tethered cows, and sailboarders must ensure that goats cannot reach their equipment!

Fort Le Marchant is the most northerly point of Guernsey and has a Napoleonic fort, which was enlarged by the early Victorians, to mark the fact. Access is across the firing range and, except when the warning flags show that the range is in use, the fort is worth the walk. It overlooks L'Ancresse Bay – the

source of much worry to the governor in 1778 and German commander in 1940. Both realised it was a perfect place for attacking armies to land and muster, so they both fortified the beach head – with defensive towers and an anti-tank wall respectively.

The latter provides shelter for the beach and a smooth surface on which to bask in the sun. The water is warm and shallow, conveniently retreating to reveal a sandy shore where children can play safey at low tide.

At the western end, Pembroke Bay is the home of a sailboarding school – the bay is sheltered from most prevailing winds, creating smooth water, but open enough to allow the gaily coloured sails to be pushed around at speed.

Behind the beach head are the club houses for the 18-hole golf course. Visitors can get temporary membership and access on certain days of the week. Part of the course is sometimes surrounded by a track used for horse racing.

The remains of the recently excavated oldest known stone construction in Europe can be seen at Les Fouaillages, access to which is from Les Amarreurs Road on the southern end of the common.

Belle Grève Bay

Map Ref: 89WV3480

Running from the marina at Salerie Corner to Richmond Point on the outskirts of St Sampson's, it can be reached from the slipways at the Longstore, Red Lion and Bulwer Avenue. Salerie Corner is a venue for year-round swimming and a popular congregating place for the sport on New Year's Day.

Belle Grève overlooks the neighbouring islands of Herm, Jethou, Sark and Jersey. The ships, fishing boats and pleasure craft which go past as they use the ports and mooring places in the area provide a source of constant interest. A mixture of rocks and sand offer plenty for children to explore, and fishing from the beach is quite good.

Hougue à la Perre, opposite the Red Lion, and a site close to La Tonnelle were sites of two Martello towers – the first demolished to make way for tram lines in 1905, the second for no apparent reason in 1959.

A generous width of sand and a sheltered position make L'Ancresse Bay popular with windsurfers, and there is a surfing school here. In the season, it is also one of the most popular beaches for families

Invaders as well as holidaymakers have been attracted to the sands of L'Ancresse – hence its many fortifications

Le Dehus Dolmen

Map Ref: 89WV3583

A Neolithic passage grave, as opposed to a true dolmen, it has four side chambers, two on each side. It is about 30ft by 11ft (at its widest point), a little over 6ft high, and covered by a mound of earth which, like the stone surrounds, is a reconstruction. Open between the hours of sunrise and sunset, it has a number of lights, with a switch close to the entrance. It is advisable to take a torch to see the nooks and crannies in shadow and in case the lights have failed. Access is from Rue des Dehus, off the junction of Grande Rue and La Rochelle Road, Vale.

The end of the chamber has several capstones. On the second from the end are the roughly carved hands and face of a figure, said to be holding a bow and arrows. The lighting is arranged to cast the best shadow to reveal it.

The tomb was excavated by Frederick Lukis in the 19th century and many of the fine pots and other artefacts found are in the Guernsey Museum. There is also a model of the tomb which is worth studying before visiting the real thing.

L'Ancresse Bay – the eastern end, close to the Common

Guernsey Candles

Map Ref: 89WV3281

This thriving business started because of a £5 candle-making kit. The founder, Peter Martel, enjoyed making decorative candles so much that he gradually switched from guesthouse proprietor to full time manufacturer. Candles are produced in two ways – either by dipping the wick into wax many times, or pouring molten wax into a mould containing the wick.

Dipped candles are given added interest by varying the colour of the wax. While hot they are carved to make intricate woven patterns. Moulds for the cast candles are made in the UK under licence. They come in a variety of shapes and sizes, depicting a range of subjects. The workshops can be walked around at leisure.

The brick kilns at Oatlands fire over 20 tons of clay a year

A rare thatched roof at Oatlands

Oatlands Craft Centre

Map Ref: 89WV3381

Built on the site of an old brickworks, the kilns of which dominate its architecture, this is the only building in Guernsey with a thatched roof. It has an Egon Ronay-recommended café – Clair's Guernsey Kitchen.

Visitors can see jewellery being made, and on sale are patchwork articles made up from designs contributed by seamstresses all over Guernsey. The bee-keeping section, with a range of different hives and equipment, includes a glass-sided beehive which is connected to the building by a short tunnel. Inside, the bees can be watched going about their daily business.

Part of the centre houses a shop selling natural products, herbs and beauty preparations while a thriving pottery produces conventional items and a number of specialist earthenware products, among them poultry casseroles and decorated plates. Perfume made in Guernsey, local herbs and beeswax candles are sold in the shop.

The craft firms based at the centre are among some of the most successful Guernsey export companies. Glass bottles blown on the site are sold to French perfume manufacturers, and paper weights, engraved tankards, glasses and sports trophies are sent worldwide.

St Sampson's

Map Ref: 89WV3481

The northern part of Guernsey, the Clos du Valle, was originally a separate island, linked with the

mainland by a bridge. When the channel was reclaimed in the early 19th century the Bridge, and St Sampson's with it, developed as a shopping centre. St Sampson's is also the industrial port of Guernsey, a major island housing area, and home to a number of boatbuilding and light industrial firms.

The northern side of St Sampson's is dominated by two large buildings, the power station, with its two huge chimneys, and a ship repair yard in which large vessels are occasionally seen. The hydrofoils which ply between the Channel Islands and St Malo can sometimes be examined at close quarters when they are beached there.

The harbour, bounded by the Bridge, North Side and South Side, is a reminder of what St Peter Port Harbour looked like before its landward ends were turned into marinas. At high tide the harbour is full of small boats, but the boats have to sit on the muddy bottom at low tide.

In winter many of these boats are removed to the Crocq, a jetty which protects the tiny innermost part of the harbour. It has a clock tower, an obelisk marked with the names of the committee who had the Crocq built in 1872, and a

Parish Churches

Many of the ancient parish churches of Guernsey and Jersey have a strong family likeness. The commonest plan has two aisles with a square tower and a plain stone spire built over the middle of one aisle. The aisles are roofed with simple stone vaults, usually plastered, and the arches between the aisles tend to be low and massive.

There are some exceptions to the common plan. Guernsey's St Pierre du Bois has three aisles, each roofed in wood, and a fine western tower with battlements, reminiscent of a Cornish church. (Look out for the modern window showing St Peter in a fisherman's guernsey).

The best Norman work is to be seen in the chancel of the Vale Church in Guernsey. Some churches have fine work in the French Flamboyant Gothic style, notably the Hamptonne Chapel (1524) in St Lawrence's Church, Jersey.

At the Reformation almost all the stained glass, the stone crosses and the fonts were removed and the wall paintings were given a coat of whitewash. Most of the current furniture and decoration is Victorian, but in the 19th century three of Jersey's medieval fonts and one of Guernsey's were retrieved

(two were found serving as pig troughs) and put back.

In both Jersey and Guernsey the civil parish is still responsible for maintaining the fabric of the church and the churchyard. Thus all ratepayers, Anglicans and non-Anglicans alike, contribute towards the cost.

A window in Vale Church with St Peter wearing a guernsey sweater

menhir which was brought to the slipway at the entrance of the jetty.

Behind warehouses on South Side stands St Sampson's Church, built on the top of a beach which has long since been reclaimed. It marks the spot where St Sampson landed and brought Christianity to Guernsey in about AD550 and, with St Brelade in Jersey, is one of two Channel Island parish churches with saddle-back steeples.

Grande Havre

Map Ref: 89WV3382

Grande Havre is a large bay created when the Braye du Valle, a channel which divided the northern part of Guernsey, was reclaimed in the early 19th century. A dyke was built from L'Islet to the Vale Church and the land between it and the Bridge, St Sampson's, reclaimed.

Standing on the dyke you can get a good idea of the area involved by looking towards the cranes which line St Sampson's Harbour wall. The 'hills' in the background are the islands of Herm and Jethou.

Grande Havre is used in a variety of recreational and professional ways. A small fleet of fishing boats takes advantage of the sheltered mooring. They are tied up in the vicinity of Les Amarreurs Bay where a small pier acts as a focal point. The fertile waters of the bay support a small oyster fishery.

There is excellent swimming from Rousse Pier on the southern side of the bay. It is particularly good at the end of a sunny summer's day when the tide is rising over hot rocks, producing warm water.

Vale Castle and Bordeaux Harbour

Map Ref: 89WV3581

St Sampson's was guarded, and is now just overlooked, by the Vale Castle. The walk to the top is steep, but the view is the best in the whole of the northern part of Guernsey. All the inhabited Channel Islands can be seen on a clear day, from Les Casquets lighthouse with its three men in the north, to Jersey with more than 80,000 souls in the south.

A recent archaeological dig revealed that this mediaeval castle was built on an Iron Age hillfort. The castle walls and the fine arched gateway date from the 15th century.

Explanatory signs around the fort point out the barracks which were built within the walls in the late 18th century, later to be used as housing between the two world wars. The cobbled roads which connected them are also shown and care should be taken when walking their uneven surfaces. The Germans added to the fortifications during the Occupation.

The castle also overlooks one of the island's most beautiful natural harbours, at Bordeaux. Crammed full of small fishing boats, Bordeaux Harbour is a delight, particularly at high tide, and was used by Victor Hugo as a setting for his novel *The Toilers of the Sea*.

Two jetties on the south side of the harbour make good swimming platforms at high tide. A pleasant beach stretches to the base of the Vale Castle and is an excellent site from which to watch boats using the harbour.

AA recommends:

L'Ancresse:
Guesthouse: Lynton Private Hotel, Hacsé Ln, *tel.* (0481) 45418

St Sampson's:
Guesthouse: Ann Dawn Private Hotel, Route des Capelles, *tel.* (0481) 25606

The entrance to Vale Castle – an early site of defence for Islanders, and one that offers superb views over the other inhabited islands

Beaucette Marina is always sheltered by the old quarry wall around it: made from a former quarry, it is just north of Bordeaux Harbour

Swimming and boardsailing from L'Islet, Ladies and Chouet beaches which circle Grande Havre are also popular.

The firm sand of Chouet beach is sometimes used for autocross.

Guernsey – Central

Parishes of Castel, St Andrew and St Saviour

Cobo Bay

Map Ref: 88WV2980

Site of a popular boardsailing school and overlooked by two hotels which provide facilities for the young set, Cobo Bay is a place at which the glamorous and would-be glamorous gather.

The seaward view is dominated by jagged red granite reefs, the only land between sunbathers and America. They also provide shelter for a small fleet of local fishing boats. One reef is marked by a pole from which a Union Jack is flown, a custom said to have been started by a fisherman whose wife's nagging drove him to spend long hours at sea. When she died, it is said, he raised the flag as a memorial, and thereafter only went to sea once a year to renew it.

Colourful sails of windsurfing rigs race in front of the rocks. The beach has lovely sand and a high sea wall to act as a windbreak; and at low tide there are gullies and rocks to explore.

Folk Museum and Saumarez Park

Map Ref: 89WV3080

Once the estate and stables of Saumarez House, the property is now the site of the Hostel of St John, an old people's home, and the Folk Museum.

The park has a wonderful collection of trees and is a popular site for youngsters as it has swings and an adventure playground. There are formal rose gardens close to the hostel and an ornamental duck pond further away in the grounds.

The park is the largest in Guernsey and site of the island's annual Battle of Flowers. The battle forms the highlight of the North Show, one of two agricultural and horticultural shows held in the park each summer.

The Folk Museum is run by the National Trust of Guernsey. Centre-pieces are the working cider press, housed in one of the barns, and a Guernsey kitchen reconstructed as it would have been more than a century ago. In the stable yard is a collection of carts, carriages and ploughs.

Le Friquet Butterfly Centre

Map Ref: 89WV3179

Although people generally know what to expect here, they still gasp as butterflies surround them for the first time. The long greenhouse in which the exotic insects are bred and released is like a tropical jungle, with brightly coloured butterflies silently flitting past to feed on nectar-bearing flowers or special containers of sugar solution.

The best time to visit the centre is on a bright sunny day. The insects need warmth to get them flying and are more active on bright days – not necessarily hot days, as Guernsey greenhouses are always warm inside if the sun is shining. The greenhouse is netted inside to prevent them from getting out.

European species of butterfly are bred on the many host plants with which the greenhouse is planted, but some of the subtropical and tropical species are imported as chrysalides which are cooled for the journey.

The chrysalides can be seen at the far end of the greenhouse where they are placed in rows, all about to hatch. None of the butterflies is deliberately killed and mounted, they live out their days in the centre.

German Military Underground Hospital

Map Ref: 89WV3076

For many of the Operation Todt slaves who built the network of tunnels, the hospital became their grave. Some idea of the difficulties, danger and hardship involved in digging the tunnels can be gained from an unfinished section at the entrance to the hospital section.

The hospital had an operating theatre, X-ray room, mortuary, kitchen, a store and dispensary. There were staff quarters, a laboratory and five ventilation shafts. But patients in the wards, taken there from the battlefields of France after D-Day, were white as sheets after six weeks and had to be taken to surface hospitals.

The entrance to the German Military Underground Hospital – built for 500 patients and large ammunition stores

Guernsey Gold and Silversmiths

Map Ref: 88WV2876

Run by Bruce Russell (who uses tools and techniques handed down by his father and grandfather) this business continues Guernsey's long tradition of skilled metalwork – a tradition that began with Huguenots coming here as exiles in the 16th century. This workshop made the silver punchbowl given by the people of Guernsey as a wedding present to the Prince and Princess of Wales, and a more recent commission was a gold castle studded with precious stones.

There is a showroom where articles can be bought, including jewellery, christening cups, Guernsey milk cans and silver ormer shells, inspired by the local shellfish delicacy. Visitors can also watch the skilled gold and silversmiths at work.

Guernsey Zoo

Map Ref: 88WV2976

Though less renowned than Gerald Durrell's establishment in Jersey, this zoo has much to offer.

Like all serious zoos, Guernsey's takes part in breeding programmes for endangered species and has its fair share of success. The first and second litters of small hairy armadillos bred in captivity were born in the zoo and director James Thomas is now an expert on these primitive animals. Education is also a major preoccupation, and school children pay regular visits, as do youth clubs and other organisations.

The zoo attempts, wherever possible, to have mixed displays of animals. No large animals are kept, except the oldest llama in captivity, which was inherited when James Thomas took over the zoo in 1975.

Among the more attractive animals are a troupe of white-lipped tamarins, short-toed otters and aviaries with spectacular collections of birds.

King's Mills

Map Ref: 88WV2978

A beautiful village at the base of the Talbot Valley, Les Grandes Moulins, as it was known, was unusual in being based on industry rather than a church, and was one

of the largest villages in the island.

Running water is scarce in Guernsey and the streams rushing down the two valleys which meet just above it were valuable sources of power. The mills, which were owned by the Crown, ground most of the flour used in Guernsey.

At the bottom of Route de la Hurette is a house called Wisteria, which is covered in the blooms in spring. It is topped by a widow's look-out from which the woman of the house would watch her menfolk coming home. Opposite is a house which makes the junction – but only just. It had the corners cut off when the two military roads were built in the early 19th century.

Little Chapel

Map Ref: 88WV2977

One of the smallest churches in the world: built by de la Salle monk Brother Deodat Antoine and modelled on the shrine at Lourdes, it was his life's work. He returned to France and died shortly after World War II broke out, before his third attempt, the one we see today, was complete.

Deodat was a member of the Brothers of the Christian Schools, who still bring parties of French children for holidays at Les Vauxbelets, the monastery at which the chapel can be found.

The woods behind the monastery were ideal for Deodat's idea, but he pulled down the first attempt after it was criticised. The second was perfect, but so small that the bishop who visited to consecrate the building could not get in, and again it was pulled down.

Tomato Museum

Map Ref: 88WV2878

The sad fact is that the presence of the museum at Kings Mills reflects the decline in a once thriving industry. Cheap Dutch and southern European imports killed the island's traditional markets in the UK and the production of 'Guernsey Toms' has dropped. Greenhouses dedicated to cultivation of different types of tomatoes using the various methods developed can be seen at the museum.

Guernsey growers first switched

Left: Guernsey Zoo has the oldest llama in captivity

Inside the Little Chapel

from grape production to tomatoes in about 1884 and the industry developed rapidly from that point. By the Occupation, when all trade ceased, production was 35,000 tons a year.

The industry picked up after the war and huge sums of money were invested in greenhouses with high light intensity designs, better methods of production and the business again flourished. The bubble burst with the increase in fuel costs in the mid-1970s and the industry has declined since.

The Tomato Museum will be of interest to the social historian and anyone who grows tomatoes at home. It has a gift shop where Guernsey tomato wine can be sampled and bought.

Le Trepied

Map Ref: 88WV2678

A Neolithic tomb some 18ft long, Le Trepied passage grave at Le Catioroc became notorious in the 17th century as the haunt of witches, said to have held their Friday night sabbaths here. Two hundred years later, the area was still avoided by respectable women.

The dolmen was extensively excavated by the 19th-century archaeologist, Frederick Lukis, one of whose sons restored the capstone. Finds included bones, arrowheads and beaker fragments,

and are in the Guernsey Museum.

One mile north stands La Longue Pierre, a 10ft menhir which can be seen from the road, with close by a 7ft stone. They may have been connected with another tomb, also excavated by Lukis but not restored.

Vazon Bay

Map Ref: 88WV2879

Shining in bright summer sunshine, this is one of the largest and most popular beaches in Guernsey. One area is reserved for surfers who take advantage of any rising tide and easterly wind when waves can provide sport the equal of anywhere in Britain.

Like many of Guernsey's bays, Vazon is popular with the ever increasing numbers of boardsailers. Fishermen too enjoy sport from the beach with big bass, mullet and plaice caught on occasions.

Vazon plays host to beach racing

A Guernsey greenhouse

on eight Saturdays during the summer and the coast road is closed to traffic for three sprint meetings. Motorcycles and cars race the clock in an event made exciting by the slight curve in the road.

The bay is a mooring for a number of fishing boats and is served by two beach kiosks at opposite ends. The south western section at Richmond is less attractive to sunbathers as it is muddy with sharp broken rocks at low tide.

AA recommends:
Castel:
Hotel: Hotel Hougue du Pommier, Hougue du Pommier Rd, 2-star, *tel.* (0481) 56531

Grand Rocques:
Guesthouses: La Galaad Hotel, Rue des Francais, Grandes Roques, *tel.* (0481) 57233 Hotel le Saumarez, Rue de Galad, *tel.* (0481) 56341

St Saviour:
Hotel: L'Atlantique, Perelle Bay, 3-star, *tel.* (0481) 64056
Self-Catering: L'Atlantique Cottages, L'Atlantique Hotel, Perelle Bay, *tel.* (0481) 64056
Guesthouse: La Girouette House Hotel, *tel.* (0481) 63269

Channel Islands Cattle

Visitors to the islands can hardly fail to notice the tethered animals which have spread the name of Guernsey and Jersey around the world. Together, the two breeds account for more people knowing about the islands than any other feature of their ways of life.

Channel Islands cows are associated with rich thick milk, wherever they are grazed. Skilful breeding and careful record-keeping have produced the two separate breeds.

The Jersey is a finely-boned animal with large, sad eyes, scalloped face and dark nose which makes it a firm favourite with visitors. In contrast, the Guernsey cow is a bigger, more solid animal. Both are a golden colour, although the Jersey ranges from brown through fawn to grey and the Guernsey often has white patches. The breeds have one common factor – their bulls are among the most dangerous in the world, and many Jersey and Guernsey cattlemen have been killed by the fierce animals.

The cattle were originally used as draught and beef animals; this was certainly the case until the start of the present century and during the Occupation. But the golden milk produced by 'Alderneys', as the Channel Island cattle were known, was ideal for making butter and the breed began to earn a reputation accordingly in the 18th and 19th centuries. They were exported in thousands to Britain and, as the breeds began to develop, importa-

tion of animals from France (from where the Channel Island cattle originate), the UK, and finally even between Guernsey and Jersey, was banned. This had the double effect of reducing the risk of cattle disease which scoured continental Europe, and maintaining the purity of the breeds. It has been illegal to import cattle into Jersey since 1789 and Guernsey since 1819. Some Charolais semen has been allowed for insemination of Guernsey cows to improve the beef stock in recent years, but the bulls produced have to be castrated and the heifers slaughtered within two years, protecting the purity of the Guernsey breed.

The islands' small fields and laws of inheritance, which tend to cause the fragmentation of land ownership, resulted in a grazing system which has charmed visitors for years. The cattle are tethered in the small fields and in summer the cows are milked where they stand. The method involves a great deal of labour as each cow needs many gallons of water each day and has to be moved several times, but it also results in close cropping of the

sward, as the animals eat grasses often left by other breeds.

This sight is becoming less common and, as dairy herds get fewer and larger, the animals tend to be taken back to stables where mechanisation has taken over. Farmers have turned from tethering to zoning fields with electric fences. But these too need frequent moving and permanent paddock systems, with the cattle released into a different area each day, are being widely adopted. The fragmented nature of the fields on some farms has been overcome by zero-grazing, when the grass is cut mechanically and fed to the cattle in their sheds or stockyards.

Milking in the fields is the traditional Channel Islands way

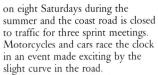

Guernsey – South

Parishes of Forest, St Martin, St Peter-in-the-Wood and Torteval

The Coachhouse Gallery

Map Ref: 88WV2876

Owned by three people, the gallery has permanent displays of work by resident artists Maria Whinney and Barry Owen Jones.

The studio also stages exhibitions of non-Guernsey artists including sculptor James Butler and Vivian Pitchforth, who paints watercolours. Dutch bronzes by Nenne van Dijk are popular, and print makers have also been shown. Sir Hugh Casson has exhibited here while president of the Royal Academy.

The light and airy gallery is in a converted barn and won a Civic Trust award.

Sheltered Fermain Bay with its sea wall and inevitable Martello tower – a superb and popular spot for swimmers

Coast Path

Map Ref: 88WV3378-88WV2375

The Coast Path stretches from St Peter Port to St Martin's Point and onwards to Pleinmont in the south-west corner of the island. The 16-mile walk is strenuous, but runs along a well-made route.

The path begins at La Valette bathing pools, rising to pass Fort George before reaching the Pepper Pot, a Napoleonic sentry box, and dipping down to Fermain Bay.

Charming little beaches are passed at Divette and Marble Bay before the path rises at St Martin's Point to join civilisation at Jerbourg. A German bunker, converted into a birdwatching hide by the Royal Society for the Protection of Birds, is passed at the Pea Stacks, with thriving seabird colonies in spring.

The path remains level until dropping to Moulin Huet and Saints Bay, and going through Icart Point to Petit Bot and Le Gouffre.

From Le Gouffre, some of the finest scenery and good wildlife are found, with ever more dramatic cliffs, Glanville fritillary butterflies flitting past, and the song of the Dartford warbler for company.

Passing the National Trust property at La Corbière, the path skirts German towers at La Prévôté and Les Tielles before dropping to 'Land's End' at Pleinmont Point.

Creux ès Faies

Map Ref: 88WV2578

This long tomb is the entrance to fairyland, according to local folklore. There are some older Guernsey people who will not go near the place, particularly at night and never when the moon is full.

It is well signposted and access is off La Rue du Braye, St Peter's. The tomb can be entered, and because it is much smaller than Le Dehus, no artificial light is needed.

Excavations revealed that it was in use between 2000 and 1800BC. A Samian sherd, now at the Guernsey Museum, was discovered along with Beaker pottery.

Fairy Ring

Map Ref: 88WV2376

Le Table des Pions as it is also known, is a circle of stones at Pleinmont Point said to have magical powers. Fairies and elves are supposed to dance around it at night wearing a path with their light footwork which never grasses over.

A meal was eaten at le Table des Pions by footmen on an ancient procession called the Chevauchée de St Michel. It was the furthest point reached by the day-long cavalcade which toured the island, inspecting the King's highways.

The pions were allowed to kiss any maiden they met on the Chevauchée, a custom which finally got the triennial march banned after the governor's wife was treated with too much enthusiasm.

Fermain Bay

Map Ref: 89WV3376

The bay is best reached by taking a ferry from St Peter Port to the large pebbled cove. A rolling jetty is pushed into the sea for passengers to disembark without getting wet.

The bay is backed by a huge sea wall topped by a pre-Martello tower. That too is overlooked – by a Napoleonic sentry box mounted on the hillside and known locally as the Pepper Pot. Well worth the walk, the inside of the tiny shelter is a spiral, beautifully capped in brick. The northern corner of Fermain is marked by concrete moorings, now seldom used by boats but popular with sunbathers and anglers.

Swimming and diving from the steep steps is excellent. So too is the swimming from the beach, although the water in Fermain is the coldest in Guernsey. The bay, however, is a sheltered suntrap and can become swelteringly hot on a sunny summer's day.

Fort Grey Maritime Museum

Map Ref: 88WV2576

A fascinating yet poignant place to visit, sad because the artefacts and pictures are from tragedies in which men and women have lost their lives around the island's coasts. Access to the museum is through a wall making part of a Martello tower built on top of the mediaeval Chateau de Rocquaine, or 'Cup and Saucer' as it is now known.

There are exhibits on some of the old wrecks. The *Prosperity*, which scattered building timber along the west coast, was a modern disaster. The biggest ship to hit Guernsey was the *Elwood Mead*, a bulk iron ore carrier on her maiden voyage from Australia; while the oil rig *Orion* drifted on to Grandes Rocques after towing ropes broke. Fortunately both were refloated and no lives were lost in either incident.

Painted white as a landmark for mariners, Fort Grey is inshore of some of the most terrible reefs in the world

The German Occupation Museum

Map Ref: 88WV2975

The museum began as a collection of souvenirs gathered together by a group of local schoolboys and stored in an attic. Ringleader Richard Heaume was to become so interested in the subject of German military artefacts that he expanded the collection until it reached such a size, importance and interest that the museum was started. It tells the story of the German Occupation, when Hitler planned to make the islands into fortresses where the Third Reich could relax. The Germans also believed that the British would go all-out to get the islands back and guns and tunnels were positioned accordingly. It was while exploring some of these tunnels that Richard Heaume found many of the things on display. A complete field kitchen was hauled out of the tunnel beneath St Saviour's Church, together with uniforms, helmets and gas masks.

Apart from German items on display, the museum features a typical Guernsey kitchen shortly after the curfew at 9pm, with a local couple listening to the London news on a secret crystal wireless.

The island was liberated on 9 May 1945, a date which is celebrated with an annual Bank Holiday, and the 40th anniversary was marked when a new hall was opened at the museum.

La Gran'mère du Chimquière

Map Ref: 89WV3276

The oldest woman in Guernsey is the finest carved menhir in Europe. She stands now outside the Church of St Martin's, which was built on an ancient site of pagan worship.

Even today, brides who marry at the church scatter flowers over her head or place a garland around the shoulders of the menhir, as she is thought to be a fertility goddess. La Gran'mère (Grandmother) was carved by Neolithic settlers in Guernsey but was almost certainly 'improved' around the time of Christ when her face, hair and headdress were modelled.

The church, which dates back to the late 12th or early 13th century and replaced an older wooden building, stands in an ancient cemetery, of which the menhir formed a part. Its outstanding feature is the porch built in the 15th century. The church was refurbished in 1869 at which time the parish authorities, who used to meet in the porch, were moved out.

Lihou Island

Map Ref: 88WV2478

Lihou is connected to mainland Guernsey by a stone causeway built by monks, who also built the now ruined priory dedicated to Notre Dame de la Roche.

The island is accessible for a couple of hours at low tide at most times of year. But crossing is dangerous if there is *any* water covering the causeway: a wicked current rips through the channel. Anyone getting cut off has to wait for the full 11-hour cycle of the tide to release them.

Lihou is about half a mile long and is owned by Mr and Mrs Robin Borwick. It can be interesting for birdwatching, swimming in the two deep pools at the western end, or just lazing.

Petit Bot Bay

Map Ref: 89WV3074

Petit Bot Bay thrives as a place for tourists to visit, but accommodation at the beautiful cove has gone, demolished by the Germans who were afraid that its two hotels might be used by British troops spying, or trying to recapture the island.

They were right to fear the clandestine use of the buildings. Operation Ambassador was the first full-blooded commando raid of World War II, and the men came ashore at Petit Port, to the west, in the middle of Guernsey's south coast. The only buildings left are a tiny cottage, a café and an 18th-century tower. The remains of a mill and waterwheel can be seen.

Most people who visit the bay are not interested in the buildings. It is one of the most popular sunbathing spots on the island, sheltered from all but the most southerly breeze.

A scene from the past – life in a typical Jersey kitchen

Traditional Farmhouses

People who know Jersey and Guernsey can flick through a magazine with property advertisements and pick out those from the Channel Islands, so distinctive is the architecture. The houses were not designed but evolved and, according to the president of Guernsey's Island Development Committee, Nigel Jee, '. . . the result was a happily-proportioned, dignified family house, not pretty in a chocolate box sense, but mature and beautiful'.

The evolution probably started with Celtic long-houses in which people and cattle lived together. Examples of 13th-century houses which may have evolved from these have been found in St Helier and at Cobo, Guernsey. The long-house developed into two-roomed houses, lofts were added and the traditional Channel Island farmhouse resulted.

This has two rooms downstairs, a living room and kitchen, with a hall between them into which the front and back doors open. The front door might have an arch and faces south. A stair tower, or 'tourelle', at the back contains stairs to the bedrooms above. The depth of the building is very close to that of the original long-house – 15 or 16ft, the length of an oak beam. The gables are very thick and each contains a carved granite fireplace.

Roofs were thatched in earlier times, although slates were used in some houses from the 17th century. A fire in the middle of the mediaeval part of St Peter Port led to a law, passed in 1683, banning thatch and giving rise to the pantiled roofscape of today. The design of the façade differs slightly between islands and according to age. The kitchen always has two windows, balanced by two in the living room on the other side of the doorway, or one window in the small parlour house. All are matched by upstairs windows, with an extra one over the door.

Facing a Channel Island farmhouse with an arched door it is easy to tell to which island it belongs. The shoulder stones in a Jersey arch have wings projecting into the wall, keying the structure in place. The Guernsey arch does not have these wings but is distinguished by a second row of stones, as large as the first, around the top. Marriage stones often form the lintel over the front door. These bear a date – often with two numbers at one end and two at the other, with syllabic initials of a couple divided by one or two interlocking hearts. These stones may commemorate a marriage, but they may also give the date the house was built or an important anniversary.

Both islands have magnificent archways in walls leading either to farms in Jersey or private estates in Guernsey.

Sausmarez Manor is Guernsey's only stately home

Rocquaine Bay

Map Ref: 88WV2577

A broad expanse of sand, interspersed with rocks, at the south-west corner of the island, it is also where the Rocquaine Regatta, one of Guernsey's most charming summer events, is held annually, early in August.

Rocquaine has the highest section of sea wall in the island, reaching 40ft in places. It was built at the end of the last century to prevent coastal erosion of false beaches created during the last Ice Age, and the wall was reinforced by the Germans during the Occupation.

The sea wall offers protection to holidaymakers and locals who use the beach. A sheltered spot close to Fort Grey provides an excellent mooring, a number of small fishing boats adding a sparkle to the summer scene.

Close to the Imperial Hotel the Rocquaine Shellfish Ponds sell

Sausmarez Manor

oysters and ormers, grown in special beds at the lowest part of the beach, and a range of live or dressed crabs, lobsters and crayfish. Shells can also be bought as souvenirs.

Les Rouvets Tropical Gardens

Map Ref: 88WV2678

A collection of subtropical and tropical plants, housed in the five greenhouses of a former tomato vinery behind Perelle Bay, it was started by an eccentric millionaire who brought the plants back to Guernsey as souvenirs of his worldwide travels.

The citrus house has a grove of standard trees on which lemon, grapefruit and several kinds of oranges grow, and is filled by the sweet smell of their flowers. The Mediterranean house has further types of oranges, begonias and red flowered pomegranate plants.

The slightly higher temperatures of the Madeira house encourage avocado pears and the 'custard apple' or pawpaw. The tropical house has pineapples and hibiscus, which reach the roof, while the desert house sees cacti blooming in the arid conditions.

Sausmarez Manor

Map Ref: 89WV3376

This has been for centuries the home of the de Sausmarez family, and is now open to the public. Earlier generations can be seen in the dining room, for the table at which living members of the family gather on special occasions is

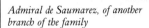

Admiral de Saumarez, of another branch of the family

surrounded by portraits of their ancestors.

The family occupied the house up to 1557, when it fell into the hands of the Andros family. Sir Edmund Andros, who was Bailiff and Lieutenant-Governor of Guernsey and also Governor of New York and Massachusetts, designed the façade. The house was bought back by John de Sausmarez in 1749, using part of a fortune amassed and left to him by his brother Philip, captain of the *Centurion*. The superb gates, with their greyhound and unicorn emblems, mark the occasion.

A tour of the house starts at the entrance porch and includes the drawing room, tapestry room, which contains the wedding suit of King James II, and the wainscot room.

The grounds, which are used for a number of charitable concerts and fêtes each year, have a miniature railway which runs through beautiful trees and shrubs.

The Strawberry Farm

Map Ref: 88WV2876

A number of greenhouses have been switched to the production of strawberries here, using a variety of cultivation methods. These include growing in long racked gutters which present the ripe fruit at a range of heights from ground level to about 6ft. Others are cultivated in growing bags which hang from the roof. The greenhouses are open to the public for inspection.

Marketing the fruit is no problem. Large numbers of tour coaches call at the Strawberry Farm and few people can resist the temptation of fresh fruit and Guernsey cream. Indeed, the demand is so great that supply has to be supplemented at the start and end of the season by strawberries imported for the farm.

Next door is the workshop of a woodcarver, where visitors can watch the craftsman and his employees making a range of items from wood bought worldwide for the business. The workshop has a display and shopping area at which mementos may be bought.

AA recommends:
Fermain Bay:
Hotels: Le Chalet, 3-star, *tel.* (0481) 35716
La Favorita, 2-star, *tel.* (0481) 35666

St Martin:
Hotels: Hotel Bella Luce, La Fosse, 3-star, *tel.* (0481) 38764
Green Acres, Les Hubits, 3-star, *tel.* (0481) 35711
Ronnie Ronalde's St Martin's, Les Merrienes, 3-star, *tel.* (0481) 35644
St Margaret's Lodge, Forest Rd, 3-star, *tel.* (0481) 35757
Guesthouse: Triton, Les Hubits, *tel.* (0481) 38017
Garage: Ruette Bray Mtrs, St Martin's, PO Box 28, *tel.* (0481) 37661

Spectacular views of Moulin Huet from the Coast Path

Alderney

Map Ref: 91WA5707

The most northerly of the Channel Islands, Alderney is perfection for many people. Alderney is slow, peaceful, picturesque and relaxing, and the Islanders welcome visitors into their community warmly, but do little to change their way of life for the tourist. Fishing, farming and finance make up the other industries, and there are a few light manufacturing and computer based workshops.

Tourists arrive from France and the UK by the yacht-full, taking a berth behind the mile-long breakwater. Others arrive by air – the Channel Islands' own airline, Aurigny Air Services, who operate the inter-island routes and fly to Cherbourg and Southampton also, are based in Alderney. Condor run a hydrofoil service from Jersey and Guernsey to Alderney twice a week in the summer, and Torbay Seaways are experimenting with a weekly ferry service from Torquay.

The island's supplies come largely from Guernsey on a coaster operated by the Alderney Shipping Company.

Visitors have all the ingredients for a relaxing holiday – long, invigorating walks, golf, sea fishing, boat trips and birdwatching. The wide sandy bays are ideal for families. When the outdoor life gets too tiring, there is the warm and ample hospitality to be had in the many bars, inns and hotels.

Farming in Alderney is a poor relation compared to that in the other Channel Islands. It is doubtful if Alderney cattle ever existed as a separate breed and certainly the island's cows are descended from Guernseys brought in after the German Occupation, when all the people and their livestock were evacuated. A few vegetables are grown and there is a herd of sheep.

Alderney's style of farming, however, is responsible for much of the wild and natural appearance which attracts naturalists and walkers. Rare birds nest, or feed in the gorse banks on migration,

butterflies flit around the island as they did in much of Britain before the use of modern pesticides, and the road verges are more like those in France than mainland Britain.

France is only eight miles away and can be seen in all but the worst visibility. Many of the professional fishermen sell their catches in Cherbourg and Cartertet, although good seafood is always available in Alderney restaurants.

Visitors can take bus tours of Alderney, and see it from 'the outside' on a boat trip which goes around the island, calling at the puffin colony on Burhou. Landing is not allowed on the island while the birds are there from April to mid-July, but they are seen in good numbers from the boat.

St Anne

Map Ref: 91WA5707

The capital of Alderney starts as you enter the cobbled Marais Square, where the history of the 'Alderney cow' can be seen over the door of the Marais Hotel. It is a fitting place to start looking at the town as it developed on the hillside close to the fields of La Petite and La Grande Blaye – farmed in ancient strip fashion until recently.

Le Huret, the ancient site of Alderney's court, leads from the square to a junction, the site of a clock tower which is all that remains of the former parish church, built in 1763. Alderney's court met in the open at Le Huret, and proclamations are read at the site to this day. The Queen's visit in 1957 is marked by a plaque on the wall.

Next to the tower is the island's

Although dairying in Alderney is less important than it was, the cows of Alderney cattle produce the same rich milk as Guernseys, from which they are descended

museum, where collections have been built up by members of the Alderney Society. After extensive renovation and the building of a new wing, the Alderney Museum was re-opened by the Queen Mother in May 1984. As you would expect from a small island, the museum is of modest size, but the quality of the exhibits is excellent.

It is divided into 12 sections, each showing a different aspect of the island. Stone and Bronze Age artefacts, including a 4000-year-old spear, are followed by Roman finds, such as pins, a buckle and ring found at the Nunnery, Longis (or Longy) Bay. The crafts and trades of Alderney are shown – dairy and fishing, farming and pottery. The German Occupation had a profound effect on the residents (all but two were evacuated to Guernsey), and relics of the sad and sickening activities of the island's three concentration camps are also on display.

Notable among the natural history exhibits are photographs of stranded whales. The museum is open from 10am until noon, Monday to Saturday.

Behind the museum, off Le Huret, lies Royal Connaught Square. It is the site of the Island Hall – formerly Government House – and leads past a number of farmhouses to the Blaye. St Anne's main shopping centre is in Victoria Street, connecting the upper town to High Street at the bottom. It passes the church, which was consecrated in 1850, a curious mixture of Norman and English styles in white Caen stone and blue local granite. Queen Elizabeth II Street, which comes off Victoria Street, is the home of the island's civil service, court and the States of Alderney. Shopping turns to recreation at the bottom of Victoria Street: Les Rocquettes leads left to Les Butes, where the island cricket teams play.

Looking towards Douglas Quay from Braye Bay

Harbour and breakwater

Map Ref: 91WA5708

Les Butes has a spectacular view overlooking the harbour and breakwater. When the wind is gale-force from the south west and a tide running, waves hit the breakwater and rise high into the air. Sometimes the mile-long structure is covered by white foam and water, with the harbour and Braye Bay sheltered behind.

Built between 1847 and 1864 as part of the general fortification of Alderney, the breakwater was to shelter a huge mooring for the Royal Navy – the cross-channel equivalent of Portland Harbour. A second arm, from Château à L'Etoc, creating a 150-acre pool, was designed but never built. The breakwater has been breached a number of times and the end section, which ran northwards, was demolished by the sea, creating a navigational hazard.

The structure needs constant, expensive repair, and a railway line from Mannez Quarry runs along it to carry stone for the job. Deep recesses were built on the harbour side to give workers (and today's walkers) shelter, should they be caught in adverse weather.

The tiny fishermen's harbour at the landward end of the breakwater is one of the most attractive in the Channel Islands. Surrounded by a

Fishing boats in harbour, with the harbour office in the distance

View of Fort Clonque from Giffoine Point

clutter of crab-pots, ropes, buoys, fenders and boats under repair, smelling rather sour from years of fish debris, and usually echoing with the sound of hammering, or the quiet throb of an engine being tested, it is a most relaxing spot. The little port is overlooked by the harbourmaster's office and the Alderney Sailing Club's premises. From there visiting vessels and yachts can be watched as they tie up to the main harbour wall and new jetty.

Beyond the harbour wall, at the end of the row of houses running down Rue de Braye, is the Douglas Quay. Built in 1763 to accommodate privateers, it now serves to shelter the sunbathers on Braye Beach.

Fortresses

Some idea of the fear which the 19th-century British had of the French can be judged by the row of 12 fortresses built from Fort Clonque along the north and east coasts of Alderney to Raz Island.

Alderney is fortunate that Captain William Jervois, a young architect, was chosen for the job of designing the forts. He had an eye for the landscape and countered the pure military requirements with aesthetic considerations. Fort Clonque, on an island under the cliffs overlooking the Swinge, has been converted into holiday flats and is almost romantic with rounded bastions, loopholes and turrets. Not so Fort Tourgis, an

extensive barracks block which he tried to hide by running one end of it into the hillside. The fort on Platte Saline beach is easily overlooked as it now serves as a sand and gravel store in the middle of the bay. Fort Doyle, overlooking Crabby Bay, was reinforced by the Germans, while Fort Grosnez protects the end of the breakwater and was started before Captain Jervois arrived.

Fort Albert is the biggest of the dozen, overlooking and protecting the harbour. Chateau a L'Etoc, behind Saye Bay, has also been converted into flats while Fort Corblets is a private house. The three forts at the eastern end of Alderney, Fort Les Homeaux Florains, on an islet near the lighthouse, Fort Quesnard and Fort Houmet Herbe, protecting the water from its position on another island, are all abandoned.

Frying Pan Battery was to protect Longis Bay and lies under Essex Castle which was used as a barracks. A small fort on Raz Island also defended the bay which was an obvious landing site for attacking armies – so much so that the Germans built a huge anti-tank wall at the top of the beach.

The Divers Inn at Braye

Entering Fort Quesnard, on the north-eastern tip of Alderney

AA recommends:
Hotel: Inchalla, St Anne's, 2-star, *tel.* (048182) 3220

Sark

Map Ref: 91WV4675

When Queen Elizabeth I granted Letters Patent to Helier de Carteret, the Jerseyman who colonised Sark, she founded the basis of a feudal society which has endured to this day. Indeed, to understand the island's way of life it has to be seen in the context of a 420-year-old system.

The laws of Sark were designed to protect the ownership of 40 parcels of land into which the island was split in 1564. Helier de Carteret took that number of men with him to form the settlement; in return for forming a militia, each was granted a perpetual lease of a piece of farmland and a section of cliff grazing called a côtil. Divorce is not allowed on the island because a man's eldest son is his heir and two sons from different marriages could contest tenancy of their late father's land. The leases cannot be split as tenants also have a seat on Chief Pleas – Sark's feudal parliament. Two tenants of the same piece of land would thus alter the constitution of Sark.

Sark is ruled by a Seigneur, the lord of the manor, and there have been 21 since de Carteret became the first. Of these, three were women, known as Dames – the last was Sybil Hathaway, grandmother of Mr Michael Beaumont, the present Seigneur.

Pirates using Sark as a base were the reason for setting up the colony – until 1564 the island was used as a stop-off place where water could be taken on board. It is an inaccessible place, surrounded by rocks and reefs, washed by tides and scoured by strong winter winds. But the land on top of its 320ft plateau is rich and fertile and the colony prospered. Helier de Carteret went

The narrow isthmus La Coupée

back to Jersey, handing over to his son Phillipe.

The Crown appointed officers to Chief Pleas – a Seneschal, or judge, Greffier, or registrar, and Prévôt, or sheriff. Chief Pleas is made up of the 40 tenants and 12 deputies who are elected to serve the population of about 550.

Respective Seigneurs, Dames and Chief Pleas have tried to keep the undesirable parts of the 20th century at bay. The island is well known for the refusal to allow cars, although tractors are used widely as farm vehicles and run-abouts. Only the Seigneur can own pigeons or an unspayed bitch. Income tax and VAT are unknown, but the island is not behind the times, and several homes have radio, television, telephone and telex communications.

Access is by boat – aircraft cannot fly over the island without permission of Chief Pleas which is granted only in exceptional circumstances such as a royal visit. Even urgent medical cases have to be taken to Guernsey by the St Peter Port lifeboat or the St John Ambulance boat *The Flying Christine*. The Isle of Sark Shipping Company operate a number of fast launches and a cargo ship to Sark. Passengers have to pay a landing tax which is included in the price of a ticket.

On arrival at Le Maseline Harbour there are two options available – a walk to the village or riding on 'the toast rack'. This 20th-century convenience is an open, bus-like carriage pulled by tractor up the steep, dusty road to the Bel Air Tavern. It is worth letting the rush of your fellow passengers leave for the village as

A tunnel leads to Creux Harbour

The old dovecote in the gardens of the Seigneurie, Sark

you explore the tiny Creux Harbour, through a tunnel to the left of the toast rack terminus at the bottom of Harbour Hill.

Horses and carriages

A number of horses and carriages wait, like cabbies, at the top of the hill to give the tour for which, rightly, Sark has become famous. Try to pick a local person, for although those who come to Sark for the season are good drivers they are not steeped in the ways of the island as are the Sarkees, who give better commentaries.

The carriages can take a number of routes around the island, and indeed can be used like taxis if you have the fare, but the usual tour heads out towards L'Eperquerie – the original landing for the settlers from 1564 onwards until the harbours were built. The view takes in the islands of Brecqhou, Herm, Jethou and Guernsey and a short stop is made to admire it. On Mondays and Wednesdays the tour stops at the superb ornamental gates at the entrance to La Seigneurie, giving time to visit the gardens – the house is closed to the public.

La Seigneurie

La Seigneurie is one of the most beautiful manor houses in the Channel Islands. It has been the home of Sark's feudal lords since 1730 when one of the three Dames, Susanne Le Pelley, bought it and gave the original manor house, Le Manoir, to the minister. The lines of the house are spoiled only by a tower from which signals were sent by the Collings family, who succeeded the Le Pelleys, to their relatives in Guernsey. Dame Sybil Hathaway wanted to demolish the tower but the cost was too high.

The house stands on the site of a monastery set up by St Magloire. A school for Norman noblemen's children, it was sacked by Norse raiders in the 9th century leaving a pile of stones and many stories which have gone into the folklore.

The gardens flourish in the protection afforded by the walls which surround them. All the Channel Islands, while almost frost-free, suffer from the blasting effect of the salt winds, and walled gardens hold the key to successful cultivation of half-hardy plants normally seen in greenhouses.

Relics of the German Occupation of Sark can be seen along with cannons and a granite cider apple crusher. The gardens also have an ornate dovecote, built in 1730 to house Dame Susanne Le Pelley's pigeons and those of subsequent seigneurs, and now home to a flock of white fantailed doves.

Little Sark

The carriages resume their tour with a long trek down Rue du Sermon to La Coupée, the isthmus which connects Sark and Little Sark. The smaller island cannot be explored on the tour but is worth visiting later if time permits. Crossing La Coupée is an ordeal for those who hate heights, but railings ensure that it is safe.

Scene of Sark's futile mining industry, the island has a few overgrown shafts, one of which is now used for dumping waste. It is an appropriate end for an industry which brought ruin to the Le Pelley family: they sank four shafts, £30,000 on wages for 250 Cornish miners imported for the venture, and eventually their feudal rights, in the search for silver, copper and lead.

The Venus Pool, a huge rock pool, is reached by passing the mines and descending the steep path – worth the trip for a refreshing swim. Point à Clouet, above the pool on top of the cliffs, has views out to L'Etac de Sark, offering a chance to see the puffins which nest on the rock, bobbing on the sea in spring. Little Sark's hotel is La Sablonnerie where, besides the good fare served to residents, meals, refreshments and cream teas can be bought.

Horse-drawn carts are the ideal way to tour Sark

The carriage ride returns down the Rue de la Coupée, passing the road to Dixcart Valley and Bay on the right and Happy Valley on the left with its views down to Hotel Le Grand Beauregard and the Pilcher Monument. The horse heads for home, turning right into Mill Lane (Rue du Moulin). A mill is passed, built at the highest point on the island to catch the wind. It was used as an observation tower by the Germans who made good use of the 365ft vantage point. It is now a three-storey gift shop. The final part of the journey either loops past St Peter's Church or goes via the Avenue to La Collinette where the ride began.

The Village

One side of The Village is formed by Rue Lucas. About 75yd from the top of the hill, a modern pottery welcomes the inquisitive, and a cycle hire shop caters for the requirements of independent explorers. A little further down Rue Lucas a right turn takes a thirsty traveller to the Mermaid Tavern.

The Village is the heart of island life, but its main street, the Avenue, is one of the least attractive parts of Sark. Running inland from the top of Harbour Hill it is spoiled by a ramshackle collection of small huts which form the shopping area. Nevertheless, it is an interesting spot where the tourists throng as they examine the duty-free goods which make Sark the cheapest place to shop in the Channel Islands.

The Avenue forks, left to Le Manoir, once the Seigneur's home,

A pair of wrought-iron gates to the Seigneurie were given to Dame Sybil on her marriage to Robert Hathaway

right to the Greffe and St Peter's Church. Opposite Le Manoir is the junior school and a tiny two-celled prison, normally reserved for those to whom the duty-free drink proves too attractive. The road past the church, which was built for £1000 in 1820, leads to the Island Hall, built by Dame Sybil to provide much needed recreational facilities. There is usually something going on in the hall and visitors are always made welcome.

The senior school is at the end of

Display of cannon in the grounds of the Seigneurie

the road, making the corner at Clos à Jaon crossroads. Rue de la Rade leads to La Seigneurie, the right turning leads to the Carrefour crossroads where another right turn leads into Rue Lucas.

AA recommends:
Restaurant: Aval Du Creux Hotel, Harbour Hill, 2-forks, *tel.* (048183) 2036

Herm

Map Ref: 90WV3980

The fifth island of the archipelago, Herm is a European desert island, a naturalist's dream and family adventure playground all in one.

A 15-minute sea crossing from Guernsey brings visitors to Herm Harbour

With no roads, let alone traffic, visitors are free to wander almost where they will, whether they are after sunbathing beaches, birdwatching walks, shell safaris or somewhere just to sit and reflect in peace and quiet.

Herm is one-and-a-half miles long and about half-a-mile wide, shaped roughly like a wedge of cheese on its side. The island has cliffs in the south and tapers to a flat area in the north. Access is by boat from St Peter Port and takes about 20 minutes. The first ferry of the day fetches the milk produced by the island's large herd of Guernsey cows. Catching it gives up to 11 hours on the island, if wanted, and is also cheaper than the other ferries which start running at about 10am.

There are four main areas of countryside. The common in the north was once much larger, stretching out over a line of rocks called the Humps. But erosion, which is still acting on the fragile sandy soil, has created a series of islands in the last few thousand years. Walking over the common without shoes is not recommended due to the presence of burnet rose, whose thorns are very painful. The remains of a 16ft-long Neolithic tomb can be seen here. The site of another one, destroyed by 19th-century quarry workers, is marked by an obelisk.

A path skirts the island passing Shell Beach and Belvoir Bay, both of which are suntraps (the sun's rays seem particularly strong in Herm, because of clear skies and the lack of car exhaust fumes). The path goes on through undergrowth, boggy areas and light woodland, which together make up Herm's main natural habitat.

The cliffs are spectacular in spring when they host large numbers of migrating birds in the natural rock gardens and flower banks, with a backdrop of deep blue sea and the other islands. Agricultural land is farmed fairly intensively to get the most from the maximum number of animals, but the skirt of scrub and wild land around the island is left alone.

Recreational activities include fishing, which is excellent from the rocks and beaches, camping on a well-equipped site, and skindiving. The island is peaceful; transistor radios are not allowed, and although many people visit each good summer day, Herm never seems to get crowded. A number of shops, a café and restaurant are available close to the harbour and the White House Hotel, opposite which is Herm's minute beehive-shaped prison.

On top of the hill stand a tiny chapel, school, Herm's power plant and a shelter where draught cattle were shod, which together make up Le Manoir Village. St Tugal's Chapel, founded by a monastic order, is more than 900 years old, and services are held by the tenant, Major Peter Wood, on most Sundays. He is often assisted by organists who volunteer for the job while staying at the hotel.

In 1920 the novelist Compton Mackenzie was the tenant. Herm was the setting for *Fairy Gold*, but he found it too large to manage, and in 1923 exchanged it for Jethou (where he spent seven happy years) before being bitten once again by wanderlust in 1930 and leaving for the Hebrides, never to return.

A row of self-catering cottages

Some Neolithic remains have survived – on Herm Common

leads to the power plant which can be detected well in advance by the throbbing of its three diesel generators. The room for Herm's seven or eight primary school children is in a courtyard behind the plant.

A large tower marks the grounds of the manor house in which the Wood family, tenants until 2029, have set up their home. Close to the wall surrounding the house and garden is a stall in which cattle were placed while they were shod. Unlike horses they cannot stand on three legs and had to be supported while the smithy did his work. The animals pulled carts containing granite which was quarried on several parts of the island.

Peter Wood, present tenant of the island of Herm

Directory

GETTING TO THE CHANNEL ISLANDS

Check with your travel agent well before your trip, because of the number and complexity of various fares available to the islands.

There are plenty of package tours available, combining reduced-fare flights with accommodation, food and sometimes car hire.

By air

Airports throughout Britain serve the Channel Islands with direct daily links to Jersey and Guernsey (and to a lesser extent Alderney) during the summer season. Also available are year-round regular connecting flights to a number of airports on the Continent, such as Dinard, Amsterdam, Zurich and Paris, reduced in winter.

UK flights are also reduced in the winter but daily flights are still maintained with airports including London Heathrow and Gatwick, Bournemouth, Manchester and Southampton.

Services operate daily in summer between Alderney and English south coast airports.

By sea

Services are liable to change: contact travel agents and tourist boards for latest information.

Passenger/car ferries operate from Weymouth and Portsmouth to both Guernsey and Jersey, daily in the summer months with a reduced service (none from Weymouth) in the winter.

In the summer there may be a weekly service from Torquay to the islands. Contact Torbay Seaways, 5 Beacon Quay, Torquay, Devon. *Tel.* (0803) 214397.

Sailings are reduced considerably during the winter and are prone to delay because of bad weather. Car/ferry services also link Jersey and Guernsey (via Jersey) with the French mainland most of the year.

There are also *fast launch* and *hydrofoil* services from the main islands to France. Day tours to French tourist ports are also available (see *Passports and Visas*).

For full details of fares, schedules and passenger information: British Channel Island Ferries, New Harbour Road South, Poole, Dorset BH15 4AJ. *Tel.* (0202) 681155.

Emeraude Ferries (car ferry service to St Malo from Jersey only), 17 Seaton Place, St Helier, Jersey; New Jetty, White Rock, St Peter Port, Guernsey.

HOW TO GET BETWEEN THE ISLANDS

By air

There are daily connecting flights between Jersey, Guernsey and Alderney throughout the summer, but the services are reduced in winter months.

These three airports are also used regularly by small private aircraft between islands and also from the UK and French mainland.

By sea

Daily *car/passenger ferry* services connect Jersey and Guernsey (services reduced in winter).
Fast launches and other vessels serve the islands from the Normandy ports of Carteret and Portbail (summer season only).

Fast *hydrofoils* (passenger only) link all the islands on certain days of the week between March and October. The service is stopped during the winter months. There are also hydrofoil links between the islands and St Malo. Check with Condor Ltd (they also offer tours from Jersey to the other islands and from Guernsey to Alderney, Jersey and France), Commodore Travel, 28 Conway Street, St Helier; New Pier Steps, St Peter Port.

No cars can be taken to the following islands:
Sark can be reached by hydrofoil direct during the summer (45 minutes from Jersey) or by fast launch from St Peter Port (about 45 minutes). Launch service: Isle of Sark Shipping Co Ltd, White Rock, St Peter Port. *Tel.* (0481) 24059.
Herm: the fast launch from St Peter Port takes about 15 minutes.
Lihou, off Guernsey's west coast, can only be reached across the causeway at low water – check local tide tables for times.
Burhou, an uninhabited bird sanctuary two miles off the north-west coast of Alderney, is approachable only in calm weather by boat, as local waters are treacherous. However, boat trips can be organised.

ISLAND TRANSPORT

Cars

Visitors can take their own cars by ferry to Jersey and Guernsey, or hire cars at very competitive rates (amongst the cheapest in Europe). There is the added advantage that petrol is far cheaper than on the mainland.

Hire rates vary according to the time of year, duration and type of car hired. Guernsey and Alderney car hire tariffs are cheaper than Jersey's.

To hire, visitors must produce a valid driving licence with no endorsements. Some firms impose a minimum age limit of 20. Some companies have a maximum age limit as well, so it is wise to check. You can pay by credit card or cheque – there is unlimited mileage and liability insurance is usually included.

Points to watch: Traffic congestion is commonplace, especially at the height of the tourist season, and visitors should be aware of narrow roads, granite walls, farm vehicles and wayward cyclists or pedestrians on winding country lanes.

Guernsey petrol stations are closed on Sundays. It is generally forbidden to drive on a beach, and filter-in-turn signs at busy intersections mean cars must alternate with those coming from other directions. In Guernsey and Alderney a large yellow arrow painted in the road indicates a give-way junction is about 30 yards away.

Parking: Apart from multi-storey car parks in Jersey, the main method of parking is either parking meters (Jersey) or street disc parking (a time disc placed in the windscreen of your car shows when you arrived). Traffic wardens are vigilant. There are no parking meters in Guernsey.

Speed limits: In Jersey, the all-island limit is 40mph, although in some areas this is cut to 20mph or even lower. Guernsey's speed limit is 35mph with signposts for 25mph or less on certain roads. In Alderney it is generally 35mph, with 20mph in town and just 12mph permitted in the town's main street.

Small vehicles

Bicycles, mopeds, motorcycles and scooters can be hired, as can tandems. Most can be hired by the day or week. For mopeds and motorcycles driving licences are required and helmets, provided by the rental company must, by law, be worn.

Public transport

There are regular *bus* services in both Jersey and Guernsey around the islands and from the airports to town. Buses run in summer in Alderney.

Taxis will take passengers all over Jersey and Guernsey, but watch out for supplements.

Coach companies operate morning, afternoon or all-day tours in Jersey and Guernsey.

In Sark, with cars forbidden, the only available vehicles apart from bicycle hire are *horse-drawn carriages* and *tractor-drawn trailers* operating from the harbour, known locally as 'toast racks'.

Alderney has the Channel Islands' only *railway*. It runs from the harbour to the quarry.

CURRENCY

Banknotes and coins
The Bailiwicks of Jersey and
Guernsey both issue their own,
which circulate between the islands
but are not accepted out of the
islands as legal tender. The notes
and coins are issued in the standard
British denominations from 1p
coins up to £50 notes, and £1 notes
are still in circulation. British money
is freely accepted, however: no need
to change money travelling from
the UK. Irish money is not
normally accepted at face value.
    All the familiar British high street
banks have branches in Guernsey
and Jersey. They are open 9.30am–
3.30pm, Monday to Friday and
some banks are open 9.30am–
12 noon on Saturdays.
    Credit cards are widely accepted.
Travellers cheques can also be used
as can Eurocards.

CUSTOMS

Passports and visas are not required
for any of the Channel Islands by
visitors from the British Isles and
the Irish Republic. Visitors from
EEC countries may travel to any of
the Channel Islands using passports.
    Should you wish to take a day
excursion to France or any
European country from the islands,
it is sensible to bring a valid
passport or British Excursion
Document, valid for one month
from the day of issue (application
forms from most travel companies
and main post offices in the United
Kingdom). You are advised to
obtain the documents *before* arriving
in the Channel Islands, because of
the formalities involved.

Animals
The islands are very conscious of
the danger of rabies and animals
may no longer be brought to the
islands other than from Great
Britain, Northern Ireland, Eire and
the Isle of Man. Yachtsmen from
these areas are not allowed to bring
animals in if they have landed
anywhere else on the way. Pet
smugglers are subject to heavy fines
and even jail sentences, and animals
are put into quarantine.

FACTS ABOUT THE ISLANDS

Jersey
About 9½ by 5½ miles. Population
over 80,000, major town is St
Helier (population 30,000).
Guernsey
25 square miles, population about
55,000, major town is St Peter Port
(population 16,000).
Alderney
3½ by 1½ miles, population about
2000.
Sark
3½ by 1½ miles, population less
than 600.
Herm
1½ miles long, population about 40
(10 families).

CALENDAR OF EVENTS

Jersey
Mar   Jersey Jazz Festival
May   Spring Festival;
            Good Food Festival Week
Jun   Festival France-Jersey;
            Open Golf Tournament
Jul   Floral Island Week
Aug   Battle of Flowers
Sep   International Folk Festival;
            Battle of Britain Week
            (including Air Display)
Oct   International Darts Festival

*Festivities at Jersey's Battle of Flowers,
the second Thursday in August*

Guernsey
May   Liberation Day Celebrations;
            International Slide
            Competition
Jun   Hash House Harriers Half
            Marathon;
            International Dance Festival
Jul/Aug
            Annual Festival of Music
Jul   Vaier Marchi;
            National Hill Climb;
            'Round Table' Harbour
            Carnival and Regatta
Aug   South Show, West Show;
            Battle of Flowers
Sep   Powerboat Week;
            Battle of Britain
Oct   International Chess Festival

Jersey/Guernsey
May   Muratti cup football match,
            hosted in alternate years by
            each island

Alderney
May (first Sun)
            Milk o' Punch Sunday
Aug (first week)
            Alderney Week

Bank Holiday is always on the first,
not the last, Monday in August.

Sark
Jun   Midsummer Show
Jul   Garden Show;
            Sark to Jersey Rowing Race
Aug   Water Carnival (two days);
            Garden and Farm Produce
            Show
Sep   Horse Show

Exact dates vary each year, so
details should be checked.

ARCHAEOLOGICAL SITES

The Channel Islands are particularly
rich in prehistoric relics and guides
are available locally. This is a
selection only. Access is unrestricted
except where stated. A torch is
useful for passage graves.

JERSEY

**GOREY (Gouray), La Pouquelaye
de Faldouet:** (buses 1 and 1a to
Gorey,then walk uphill), Neolithic
dolmen, approached through avenue
of trees from Rue des Marettes.

GROUVILLE, La Hougue Bie:
(bus 3a), 40ft mound housing
superb 50ft-long Neolithic passage
grave (lit) of 3000BC, surmounted
by mediaeval chapels. Site includes
museums. Open March to October,
Tuesday to Sunday, 10am to 5pm
(and by appointment). Admission
charge. Grounds and ground floors
suitable for disabled people.

**ST MARTIN, Le Couperon
Dolmen:** (buses 3 and 3b to top of
Rozel Hill), gallery grave developed
from 2000-year-old passage graves.

ST OUEN, Dolmen des Monts:
(bus 9 to St Ouen's Church, then
walk west past church and take first
right. Bear left into Rue de Grantez
and left into Le Chemin des Monts.
After ¼ mile follow track to left).
Neolithic passage grave in National
Trust land.
Grosnez Castle: (bus 9a), ancient
ruin high on rugged cliffs.

GUERNSEY

ST PETER'S, Creux ès Faies:
(off La Rue du Braye), said to be
door into fairyland; finds date from
around 2000BC.

**ST SAVIOURS, Le Trepied
Passage Grave and La Longue
Pierre Menhir:** (buses E1 and E2;
southern point Perelle Bay, access
by path from Le Catioroc car park),
single-chambered tomb, some 18ft
by 6½ft, 4ft 4in high. About a mile
north beside a private drive to Fort
le Crocq, La Longue Pierre Menhir
– a 10ft standing stone – can be
seen from the public road.
Le Dehus: (off La Roche road),
spectacular Neolithic passage grave
(always lit), with unique carvings.
La Varde: (on hill between
Pembroke bus terminus and Chouet
car park), Neolithic passage grave
some 40ft by 12ft.
Les Fouaillages: (signposted from
Les Amarreurs Road, L'Ancresse),
important Neolithic and later burial
site excavated and preserved for
view.

CASTLES, MUSEUMS AND ATTRACTIONS

JERSEY

**GOREY, ST MARTIN, Mont
Orgueil Castle:** (buses 1, 1a and 2),

with defence works from the 13th century to the last war in spectacular position. Tableaux with commentary. Open seven-day week March to October, 9.30am to 5.30pm. Admission charge.

MILLBROOK, ST LAWRENCE, The Glass Church: (buses 8, 9, 9a, 12, 12a, 14, 15, 17; next to Coronation Park), transformed by glasswork of French Master René Lalique. Donations appreciated.

ST CLEMENT, Samarès Manor Estate: (bus 19 to Marine Avenue), seigneurial manor in beautiful grounds famous for plant collections. House open end April-September. Grounds open daily April to Christmas, 10am to 5pm (not Sunday). Admission charge. Suitable for disabled people.

ST JOHN, Heatherbrae Farm: (bus 5), working Jersey-herd dairy farm. Open May to September, Monday to Saturday, 2.30 to 5.30pm. Admission charge.

ST HELIER, Elizabeth Castle and Hermitage: (ferry, or walk at low tide), 16th-century island castle and oratory to 6th-century St Helier. Open late March to October. Admission charge.
Fort Regent: shell of 23-acre Napoleonic fort converted into giant leisure centre offering sport, entertainments and refreshments. Open daily 9am to 11pm for sports; 10am to 10pm (high season) and 10am to 6pm (low season) for exhibitions, museums and entertainment. Admission charge. Suitable for disabled people.
Island Fortress Occupation Museum: (9 The Esplanade; 50yds from bus terminus), armaments, documents, uniforms, etc relating to German Occupation. Open daily 10am to 10pm.
The Jersey Museum: (Pier Road), history, natural history, German Occupation, etc. Open Monday to Saturday, 10am to 5pm. Admission charge.

ST LAWRENCE, German Military Underground Hospital: (Meadowbank), huge, subterranean complex built by slave labour. Open mid-March to early November, 9.30am to 5.30pm; winter Thursdays 12 to 5pm, Sundays 2pm to 5pm; closed three weeks in January. Admission charge. Suitable for disabled people.

ST MARY, Grève de Lecq Barracks: (buses 7b and 8), displays in 19th-century barracks restored by National Trust. Open late May to mid-October, Tuesday to Sunday, 10am to 5pm. Admission charge. National Trust shop.
Haute Tombette Jersey Butterfly Centre: (bus 7), butterfly 'safari' in old carnation nursery. 17th-century farmhouse and natural history display. Open daily 9am to 6pm.

Stirring the rich Jersey milk at Heatherbrae Farm

Free admission to grounds; admission charge for free-flying areas.
La Mare Vineyards: (buses 7 and 7b), wine- and cider-producing estate with restored 18th-century farmhouse and displays. Open May to early October, Monday to Friday, 10am to 5.30pm. Admission charge.

ST OUEN, Battle of Flowers Museum: (bus 9a to Five Roads), floral floats from Battle of Flowers. Open seven-day week February to November, 10am to 5pm. Admission charge. Suitable for disabled people.
St Ouen's Manor grounds: (buses 9 and 9a), grounds only of manor house, home of the de Carterets, Seigneurs of St Ouen, for 850 years. Open Tuesday 2 to 6pm. Admission charge.
Shire Horse Farm Centre: (bus 9a; Camp Donne, Route de Trodez), animals, tackle and vehicles, museum and carriage rides. Open seven-day week. 10am to 6pm. Admission charge.

ST PETER, Jersey Motor Museum: (buses 9 and 9a; in car park opposite St Peter's Church), old military and civilian cars, plus other transport. Open daily March to November, 10am to 5pm. Admission charge. Suitable for disabled people.
St Peter's Bunker: (buses 9 and 9a; in car park opposite St Peter's Church), Occupation relics. Open March to November, 10am to 5pm. Admission charge.
Sunset Nurseries: (The Flower Centre, Five Mile Road, St Ouen's Bay), exotics, plus tropical gardens, passion-flower maze and glasshouse displays. Open all year 10am to 5pm. Admission charge.

ST PETER'S VALLEY, ST PETER'S Fantastic Tropical Gardens: (bus 8; west of St Helier on Inner Road to Bel Royal), restored oriental gardens and exotic displays. Open seven-day week, from 9.30am.
Le Moulin de Quetivel: (as above). Working watermill on 600-year-old site. National Trust. Open April to September, Tuesdays and

Wednesdays, 10am to 4pm. Admission charge. Suitable for disabled people. National Trust shop.
Strawberry Farm: (as above), parkland in strawberry fields, with craft centre. Occupation bunker and model village. Open seven-day week from 9am. Admission charge to bunker museum.

TRINITY, Jersey Zoo Park and Wildlife Preservation Trust: (Les Augres Manor; buses 3a and 3b). Centre of breeding programme for hundreds of endangered species. Trust established by zoologist and author Gerald Durrell. Open all year, 10am to dusk. Admission charge.

GUERNSEY
CASTEL, Folk Museum: (Buses F and N; Saumarez Park), domestic items through the ages in old farmhouse, with larger items and vehicles in the courtyard. All in beautiful park. Open April to October, 9am to 5pm. Admission charge.
Le Friquet Butterfly Farm and Flower Centre: (buses N, F and G; Le Friquet Road), free-flying European and exotic butterflies under glass. Flower centre and amusements. Open Easter to October, 10am to 5pm. Admission charge. Suitable for disabled people. Refreshments.
Tomato Centre: (buses E1 and E2), living museum of tomato cultivation and development. Open in summer 9am to 5.30pm. Admission charge.

FOREST, German Occupation Museum: (buses C1 and C2; behind Forest Church). Occupation relics and Occupation kitchen tableau. Special tours through underground fortifications. Open Thursday to Sunday, November to March, 2 to 5pm; April to October, 10am to 5pm. Admission charge. Ground area only suitable for disabled people.

ST ANDREW, Guernsey Zoo: (buses D1, D2 and N; La Villiaze),

Ripening Guernsey tomatoes, crated and ready for export

small mammals and birds. Open daily from 10am to 6pm summer (last admission 5pm), 10am to 4pm winter. Admission charge. Suitable for disabled people.
Rose Centre: (off Candie Road), working commercial rose nursery. Open 10am to 5pm (not Sunday).
The Little Chapel: (buses D1 and D2), tiny grotto built as replica of Lourdes. Unrestricted access.
The German Military Underground Hospital and Ammunition Store: (buses D1 and D2; La Vassalarie), subterranean maze of concrete tunnels and chambers built in 3½ years by slaves. Open daily April and October 2 to 4pm, and May to September 10am to 12 noon and 2 to 5pm. Admission charge. Suitable for disabled people.

ST MARTIN, Sausmarez Manor: (bus B), only stately home in Guernsey, on 700-year-old site. Fully furnished with period pieces, fine grounds have amusements, model village and Tudor barn with train layout. House open June to October, Wednesday–Friday. Outside attractions daily in summer 10am to 6pm, and winter afternoons Thursday, Saturday, Sunday. Admission charge.

ST PETER PORT, Aquarium: (St Peter Port Steps). Tropical and cold-water fish in large tanks. Open 10am to 5pm in summer. Admission charge.
Castle Cornet: ancient castle that has seen military action from the 12th to 20th centuries. Contains displays of uniforms and other militaria. Open daily April to October, 10.30am to 5.30pm. Admission charge.

Guernsey Museum and Art Gallery: (Candie Gardens). Guernsey history, with art gallery and audio-visual theatre. Open daily 10.30am to 5.30pm, or 4.30pm in winter. Admission charge. Suitable for disabled people.
Hauteville House: (38 Hauteville), home of Victor Hugo, with fine collection of china and art. Open April to September, 10 to 11.30am, 2 to 4.30pm and in winter once a day at 10.30am for guided tour, or by appointment. Admission charge. Not suitable for disabled people.
St James Concert and Assembly Hall: (College Street), cultural centre. Details of events and exhibitions given in a regular leaflet.

ST SAVIOURS, Hanging Strawberry Farm: (buses D1 and D2), tearooms with hundreds of hanging baskets. Many other amusements and diversions. Open all year. No admission charge.
Guernsey Herb Garden: (Ashcroft Hotel, Sous L'Eglise), opportunity to wander amongst culinary, medicinal and aromatic herbs. Open May to October, 10am to 5pm. No admission charge.
Les Rouvets Tropical Vinery and Garden: (Perelle, lower end of Rue de L'Arquet), four greenhouses full of exotic blooms and plants such as coffee, tea, lemon, etc. Lakeside walk. Open daily in season, 10am to 5pm. Admission charge.
St Appoline's Chapel: (¼ mile inland from Perelle Bay), restored chantry chapel with late 14th-century fresco of the Last Supper. Unrestricted admission.

ST-PETER-IN-THE-WOOD, Fort Grey Maritime Museum: (buses C1 and C2), in 19th-century Martello tower standing on small islet in Rocquaine Bay. History of shipwrecks round Guernsey. Open summer 10.30am to 12.30pm, 1.30 to 5.30pm. Admission charge.
Orchid Fields: (buses C1 and C2; Rue des Vicheries), wet meadows behind shingle bank, habitat of some 90 per cent of Britain's *Orchis laxiflora* (loose-flowered orchid; blooms May). Unrestricted access, but membership of *La Société Guernesiaise* encouraged. Parking L'Eree Headland (not on shingle).
Silbe Nature Reserve: (buses D1 and D2), three fields with a stream and pond in the Quanteraine Valley, protected as an excellent example of a west-coast island valley. Open all year round. Unrestricted access, but membership of *La Société Guernesiaise* encouraged. Parking at green by St Peter's Church.

ALDERNEY
Alderney Museum: Old School, High Street. Island history, natural history, the German Occupation, etc. Open Monday to Saturday, 10am to 12.30pm. Admission charge.

FOOD
Fresh local fish and seafood delicacies range from freshly caught chancre and spider crabs to conger, bass, lobster, sole and plaice. One rare delight is the ormer – taken from these waters and which can be found only in one other part of the world.

All kinds of vegetables are grown locally, but probably the most famous are the Jersey Royal new potatoes. Tomatoes and kiwi fruit are mass produced under glass in Guernsey.

Milk, butter and cream are a must to try, as is the Jersey Wonder (a sort of doughnut twisted into a figure of eight), 'fiottes' (pastries) and the Guernsey gâche (a type of rich fruit loaf).

LANGUAGE
English is the main language in all the Channel Islands, but all are proud of their Norman heritage and some of the older inhabitants in Jersey, Guernsey and Sark still speak in their local patois, based on Norman French. It is incomprehensible to visitors but many Islanders do speak basic French as well.

POSTAGE AND TELEPHONES
Post offices and mail United Kingdom stamps are not valid on outgoing mail. From Jersey, only Jersey postage is valid and from Guernsey, Alderney, Sark or Herm, only Guernsey issued stamps can be used. Jersey post boxes are red, in Guernsey they are blue.

Postage rates are cheaper than in the United Kingdom and both main post offices in St Helier and St Peter Port have philatelic bureaux with local stamps for collectors, first-day covers and exhibitions. Alderney post office is a sub-post office of Guernsey.

Telephones Public telephone boxes are yellow and can be used to make local or international calls.

RADIO, TV AND NEWSPAPERS
Both Jersey and Guernsey have their own local BBC **radio** stations, and other BBC or Continental radio services can be picked up as normal or relayed by transmitter. All four British television channels are also relayed and Channel Television on ITV or Channel 3 has local news, feature programmes and documentaries.

Newspapers and magazines are flown in to the islands daily from the mainland (weather permitting) and there are two main local newspapers, the *Jersey Evening Post* and the *Guernsey Evening Press*. Alderney's local news comes in the *Journal*. Other supplements, journals and locally produced publications are also available both to locals and visitors.

SHOPPING

No VAT and low duties on luxury items makes shopping in the Channel Islands attractive. But it is always worth visitors comparing prices to make sure they are getting genuine bargains. Customs restrictions apply for visitors re-entering the UK.

Drinks, tobacco, luxury goods Alcohol is an obvious choice to take home. Prices may be higher than at duty-free shops, but the choice is wider. Locally produced wine and liqueurs can be bought. Tobacco is cheap, as are cigarettes and cigars, luxury items like jewellery (gold chain is sold by the yard), cosmetics and perfume. Scents are made in the Channel Islands based on local wild flowers and lavender.

Clothes and gifts The islands have local potteries where you can visit and buy items and there are other craft centres as well. Locally produced traditional knitwear – the fishermen's guernseys, jerseys, bretons and alderneys – is world famous and a popular buy.

For unusual souvenirs try intricate candles, walking sticks made out of locally grown giant cabbage stalks, or miniature copper milk cans. There are also bargains in electrical goods, cameras, watches, sports equipment, some clothes, china and glass.

Both Guernsey and Jersey have markets full of fresh local produce (see *Food*). Flowers grown on the islands, such as carnations, roses and freesias, can be posted home.

Early closing Most shops open between 9am–5.30pm, except for early closing on Wednesday (Alderney) and Thursday (Jersey and Guernsey). Some of the small shops in the islands close at lunchtime too. In the holiday season shops are open late at night.

CRAFT CENTRES

JERSEY

Gorey Village (Gouray), Grouville; *Jersey Pottery* (buses 1 and 1A; shop also at 1 Bond St, St Helier), hundreds of different designs. Open 9 to 5.30 weekdays, closed weekends and Bank Holidays. Suitable for disabled visitors.

L'Étacq, St Ouen; handtooled leather belts made on the spot at *Leatherland* (bus 12A). Other leather goods, plus engraved glassware. Open seven-day week.
L'Étacq Woodcrafts (bus 12A; shops also Central Market and de Gruchy's Arcade, St Helier), objects in wood, the stems of the giant (16ft) Jersey cabbage. Associated studios offer other hand-made goods. Open all year.

Mont Les Vaux, St Brelade: *The Red Barn* (440yds up hill from St Aubin), woollens, including jerseys,

guernseys and bretons.
Open all year.

Portinfer, St Ouen: *Plemont Candlecraft* (buses 9 and 9a), cottage industry, uses old methods to decorate and carve candles.
Open daily 9.30am to 5.30pm.

St Clement, Samarès Manor Estate: *The Herb Shop* (bus 19; in the manor gardens, Inner Road), herbal products including cosmetics, remedies and pot-pourri.
Open April to October (no entrance fee for shop only).

St Helier, *The Jersey Wool Shop* (2 Charing Cross), woollens, including jersey and guernsey styles.
Open all year.
The Jewellery Workshop (8½ Burrard Street), jewellery made on premises.
Open all year.

St Peter's Valley, St Peter: *The Strawberry Farm*, craft centre with glass-blowing and pottery.
Open seven-day week, from 9am.

Sion, St John: *John McCourt & Son Craft Centre* (Old Church House, Route de St Jean) includes diamond-cut glassware made on premises. Commissions taken.
Open 9.30am to 5.30pm (not Sunday).

GUERNSEY

Le Gron, St Saviours: *Guernsey Gold and Silver Smiths* (buses D1 and D2), gold and silversmithing in workshops, showroom.
Open 9am (demonstrations usually 10.45am) to 5pm (not Sunday).

Les Islets, St Peter's: *Coach House Gallery* (buses C1 and C2), paintings, prints, pottery and sculpture. Etching pottery in studios.
Open daily 11am to 5.30pm.

Les Petites Capelles, St Sampson: *Guernsey Candles* (buses H1 and H2), candlecraft exhibition and shop. Open 9am to 9.30pm summer, 9am to 5.30pm winter.

Lex Vauxbelets, St Andrews: *Guernsey Clockmakers* (buses D1 and D2; Little Chapel), workshop,

showroom and shop.
Open daily 8am to 5pm.

Rocquaine, St Peter's: *Guernsey Coppercraft Centre and Pottery* (buses C1 and C2; opposite Fort Grey), copper and brass work displayed and made to order, including island's traditional milk can.
Open summer 9.30am to 5.30pm daily; winter 8.30am to 5.30pm Monday to Friday.

St Andrews: *Les Ruettes Pottery* (buses D1 and D2 to Bailiff's Cross), traditional and modern ware.
Open 9am to 5.30pm.

St Peter Port: *Guernsey Toys* (25/27 Victoria Road), soft toys made on premises.
Open 9am to 5.15pm (except 1 to 2pm lunch; not Sunday).

St Sampson: *Guernsey Knitwear* (6 The Bridge), guernsey jumpers, cardigans and other hand-made garments.
Oatlands Craft Centre (buses L1, L2 and N; Braye Road), glassblowers, potters, jewellers, patchworkers and others in converted brickworks and farm. Glass-sided beehives.
Open 10am to 5.30pm daily in summer, closed Sunday in winter.

St Saviour: *Guernsey Woodcarvers* (buses D1 and D2), woodcarvers and shop.

SPORT

Sport plays a major role in the islands' lifestyle, both on the water and off it. For information on sports not listed here, contact local tourist boards.

Angling
An exceptional variety and number of fish abound in Channel Island waters. Anglers can fish from piers, harbour walls, beaches, breakwaters, rocks or even over a wreck. Freshwater anglers (both fly and coarse fishing) can get temporary membership of club waters at local reservoirs, ponds or abandoned quarries. Rods and reels and other

A fine catch! Sea fishing is popular in Channel Island waters

Riders are well-served by the many stables and riding centres in the islands

angling tackle (both for sea and freshwater fishing) can be hired and bait is available from most tackle shops.
Wreck fishing. Contact Dougal Lane, Melbourne Cottage, Valnord Hill, St Peter Port, Guernsey. *Tel.* (0481) 27161.
Deep sea fishing trips can be organised and leave from both Jersey and Guernsey's main harbours. Local sea angling clubs run both shore and boat angling festivals in the summer as well as fishing trips. For information on all aspects of angling in Jersey contact Mr R G Smith, c/o Wheways, 16 Broad Street, St Helier. *Tel.* (0534) 20194 (send sae).

Flying
For tuition and flying lessons apply to the CI Aero Club, St Peter, Jersey. *Tel.* (0534) 43990; Guernsey Aero Club, La Planque Lane, Forest. *Tel.* (0481) 65267/65254. Alderney Flying Club. *Tel.* (048182) 3478.

Golf
An increasingly popular sport in the Channel Islands with Jersey's Open Tournament attracting top British and European players in June. In Jersey booking is strongly advised on all courses, particularly at both 18-hole courses (open to visitors who are members of a recognised golf club). It also offers two nine-hole public courses. Contact La Moye Golf Club, St Brelade. *Tel.* (0534) 43401 or the Royal Jersey Golf Club, Grouville. *Tel.* (0534) 54416, which offers a seaside course alongside Grouville Bay.
    Guernsey has an 18-hole seaside course, also available for temporary membership, as is the nine-hole course at the St Pierre Park Hotel. Contact the Royal Guernsey Golf Club, L'Ancresse, Vale. *Tel.* (0481) 47022 and L'Ancresse Golf Club which uses the same 18-hole links course as above. *Tel.* (0481) 46523.
    Alderney Golf Club has a lovely scenic nine-hole course available to both local residents and visitors.

Tel. (048182) 2853
    There are also facilities for mini-golf, putting greens and a golf driving range.

Horse racing
There are about eight races a year at Les Landes, Jersey. Race meets are also held at L'Ancresse in Guernsey.

Horse riding
Schools on Jersey, Guernsey and Sark provide tuition and escorted hacks or treks.

Indoor sports/leisure centres
There are extensive sports facilities at the islands' two big leisure complexes: Fort Regent in St Helier and Beau Sejour in St Peter Port.

Motor racing
In Jersey events organised by the Motorcycle and Light Car Club take place at St Ouen's Bay and Bouley Bay Hill. In Guernsey motor racing at Vazon Bay is organised by the Guernsey Kart and Motor Club. *Tel.* (0481) 26986.

Sailing
Experienced yachtsmen visit the Channel Islands from all over the world. But there are facilities for beginners with local yacht clubs and dinghy sailing schools.
    More experienced sailors can charter yachts from companies in both Guernsey and Jersey to sail round the islands or to mainland France. There are marina facilities in Jersey, Guernsey and Alderney. Please note that these waters aren't easy, and those round Alderney are notorious.
    For Jersey, contact the Royal Channel Islands Yacht Club, St Aubin. *Tel.* (0534) 45783. St Helier Yacht Club, South Pier. *Tel.* (0534) 21307/32229. For Guernsey, contact Royal CI Yacht Club, St Peter Port. *Tel.* (0481) 25500. For Alderney, contact the Alderney Sailing Club. *Tel.* (048182) 2758.

Sub aqua and snorkelling
The clean waters around the islands have always attracted divers.

Tuition is available, equipment can be hired and experienced divers can join local expeditions to study marine life, rocks or war relics. Currents and tides make local advice on where to dive essential. The Jersey Sub Aqua Club and British Sub Aqua Club can be contacted at La Folie Inn, South Pier, St Helier.
In Guernsey, contact the Blue Dolphin Sub Aqua Club. For further information contact the relevant tourist boards.

Surfing
St Ouen's Bay, Jersey, has hosted championship events. Both boards and wetsuits can be hired and lessons are available from surfing schools. In Guernsey the best surfing beach is Vazon Bay.

Swimming
Beaches are beautiful anywhere in the Channel Islands for swimmers and family fun. But a note of caution – bathers should beware of the tides (Channel Islands tide movements are among the largest in the world), and the danger of submerged rocks and currents in unfamiliar waters. If in doubt find out when and where to swim.
    Some of the more popular beaches in Jersey are patrolled by beach guards and have safe bathing areas marked by flags, with amenities on-shore for visitors. There are fully-equipped indoor swimming pools and sports facilities in both Jersey and Guernsey leisure centres.

Water-skiing
All facilities, equipment and instruction are available from qualified instructors in both Jersey and Guernsey. In Jersey, St Aubin's Bay (La Haule) and St Brelade's Bay are the main centres.

Windsurfing
Windsurfing instruction is available in Jersey, Guernsey and Alderney, and all kinds of sailboards are available. Tuition is available for children and beginners upwards. Guernsey is an internationally known centre for the sport.
    Contact Jersey Wind and Water Windsurfing Schools at St Aubin and St Brelade's Bay. *Tel.* (0534) 42188 or 43777. In Guernsey, contact Windsurfing International, Cobo. *Tel.* (0481) 53313.

TOURIST INFORMATION
Jersey Tourism Office, 35 Albermarle Street, London W1X 3FB.
Jersey States Tourism Committee, Weighbridge, St Helier, Jersey, Channel Islands.
Guernsey States Tourist Board, PO Box 23, White Rock, St Peter Port, Guernsey.
Alderney States Tourist Office, Alderney.
Sark Tourism, The Information Centre, Sark.

CHANNEL ISLANDS

Atlas

The following pages contain a legend, key map and
atlas of the Channel Islands, three motor tours
and fifteen island walks.

Above: La Coupée, Sark

Channel Islands Legend

GRID REFERENCE SYSTEM

The map references used in this book are based on the Universal Transverse Mercator Grid, correct to within 1000 metres. They comprise two letters and four figures, and are preceded by the atlas page number.

Thus the reference for St Helier appears 86 WV 6548

86 is the atlas page number

WV identifies the major (100km) grid square concerned (see diag)

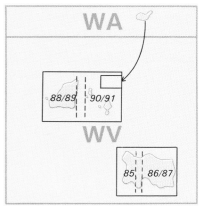

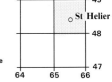

6548 locates the lower left-hand corner of the kilometre grid square in which St Helier appears

65 can be found along the bottom edge of the page, reading W to E

48 can be found along the right-hand side of the page, reading S to N

WALKS AND TOURS (All Scales)

   Start point of walk

   Route of walk

   Line of walk

   Alternative route

   Start point of tour

   Route of tour

   Featured tour

ORIENTATION

True North
At the centre of the area is 11½ 'E of Grid North

Magnetic North
At the centre of the area is about 5°W of Grid North in 1989 decreasing by about ½° in three years

ATLAS & TOURS 1:50,000 or 1¼ " to 1 MILE

ROADS , RAILWAYS AND PATHS

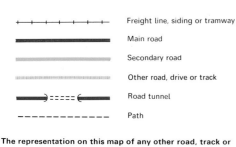

┼┼┼┼┼┼┼┼   Freight line, siding or tramway

   Main road

   Secondary road

   Other road, drive or track

   Road tunnel

– – – – – – – –   Path

The representation on this map of any other road, track or path is no evidence of the existence of a right of way

BOUNDARIES

— — — — — — —   Parish

GENERAL FEATURES

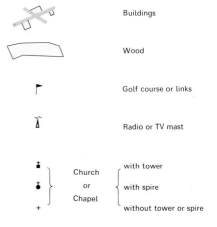

   Buildings

   Wood

   Golf course or links

   Radio or TV mast

   Church
   or   with tower
   Chapel   with spire
            without tower or spire

Compiled from Ministry of Defence, United Kingdom mapping at 1/10 000, 1/10 560 and 1/25 000 scale, dated 1965-1975

WATER FEATURES

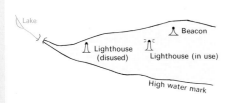

Lake

Beacon

Lighthouse (disused)   Lighthouse (in use)

High water mark

ANTIQUITIES

VILLA   Roman
Castle   Non-Roman

+   Position of antiquity which cannot be drawn to scale

⚔ 1066   Site of battle (with date)

✷   Tumulus

JERSEY & GUERNSEY WALKS
1:25,000 or 2½ " to 1 MILE

TOURIST INFORMATION

Bus Terminus

Camp Site (Caravans and Motor Caravans are not permitted)

P Car Park (public)

P Car Park (private)

i Information Centre

— — — Recommended Walk

Picnic Site

Pottery Selected places of interest

Public Convenience

Viewpoint

Public Telephone

ROADS AND PATHS

JERSEY   GUERNSEY

Main road
Secondary road
Other road, drive or track
Loose surface
Path

ABBREVIATIONS

CH	Club House	PC	Public Convenience
F Sta	Fire Station	PH	Public House (Rural Areas)
FB	Foot Bridge	PO	Post Office
F	Fontaine	Pp	Pump
G	Garage	Sch	School
Liby	Library	T	Telephone (public)
MS	Mile Stone	T(A)	Telephone (AA)
Mus	Museum	Twr	Tower
PBS	Parish Boundary Stone	TH	Town Hall

BOUNDARIES

— · — · — Parish

· · · · · · · · · Vingtaine

VEGETATION

JERSEY   GUERNSEY

Coniferous trees
Non-coniferous trees
Orchard
Scrub
Rough grassland

GENERAL FEATURES

DANGER AREA — Ranges in the area

Church or chapel: with tower / with spire / without tower or spire

Lighthouse; beacon

△ Triangulation station

Water

Sand, sand & shingle

Quarry

Refuse tip

Sloping masonry
Site of antiquity
Bus or coach station
Glasshouse

HEIGHTS

JERSEY
Contours are at 20 feet vertical interval

GUERNSEY
Contours are at 10 metre vertical interval

HERM WALK
1:10,000 or 6 " to 1 MILE

ROADS & PATHS

Road
Track
Footpath

Where unfenced shown by pecked lines.

VEGETATION

Rough grassland
Scrub
Woods

HEIGHTS

Contours
Triangulation station △
Surface height 65.8 ·

Contours are at 5 metres vertical interval

GENERAL FEATURES

Quarry
Boulders
Reservoir
Rocks
Sand and shingle
Roofed Building
Glasshouse
Ruin ⊠

SARK WALK
1:10,560 or 6 " to 1 MILE

Road, (with Mileage Indicator)
Road, Privately Maintained
Track
Footpath
Rocks, Boulders
Sand and Shingle
Cliff and Scarp
Stream and Pond
Woodland
Contours 310 300 290
Low Water Mark LWM
Public or "Tenement" Building
Freehold or Other Building
Cemetery
Spot Height (Values in Feet) · 356

ALDERNEY WALK
1:10,560 or 6 " to 1 MILE

Road
Track Tk
Path Path

Where unfenced shown by pecked lines.

Roofed Buildings
Glasshouse
Ruin ⊠
Triangulation Station △
Sand Pit
Other Pits
Quarry
Boulders
Contours (10 feet vertical interval)
Surface Heights · 165

Trees, Non Coniferous
Orchard
Scrub
Saltings
Rough Grassland
Direction of flow of water Shingle / Sand

ABBREVIATIONS

Church	Ch	School	Sch
Cart Track	CT	Telephone Call Box	TCB
Defence Works	Def Wks	Vicarage	Vic
Foot Bridge	FB	Well	W
Post Office	PO		

Key to Atlas pages

Distances in miles to ST HELIER AND ST PETER PORT		
	Map Ref: 86 WV 6548	Map Ref: 89 WV 3378
	St Helier (Jersey)	St Peter Port (Guernsey)
Torquay	115	86
Weymouth	109	75
Portsmouth	144	122
Cherbourg	74	54
St Malo	44	64

ENGLAND

English Channel

CHANNEL ISLANDS

FRANCE

0 Kilometres 5 10
0 Miles 5

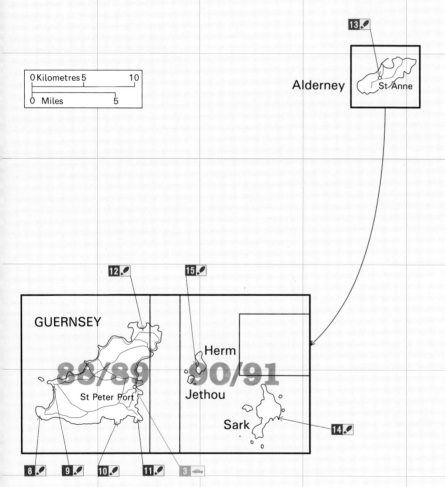

13 Alderney — St Anne

12 **15**

GUERNSEY

88/89

St Peter Port

90/91

Herm

Jethou

Sark

14

8 **9** **10** **11** **3**

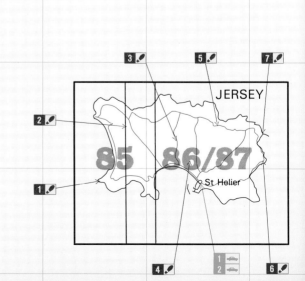

WALKS FOR CHANNEL ISLANDS
Jersey Walk 1 La Corbière
     Walk 2 St Ouen
     Walk 3 St Lawrence
     Walk 4 St Helier
     Walk 5 Trinity
     Walk 6 Gouray
     Walk 7 St Martin
Guernsey Walk 8 Pleinmont
     Walk 9 L'Erée
     Walk 10 Icart Point
     Walk 11 Jerbourg
     Walk 12 L'Ancresse Common
Alderney Walk 13 St Anne
Sark Walk 14 Creux Harbour
Herm Walk 15 Herm Harbour
TOURS FOR CHANNEL ISLANDS
Jersey Tour 1 St Helier
    Tour 2 St Helier
Guernsey Tour 1 St Peter Port

3 **5** **7**

JERSEY

2

85 86/87

St Helier

1

4 **1** **2** **6**

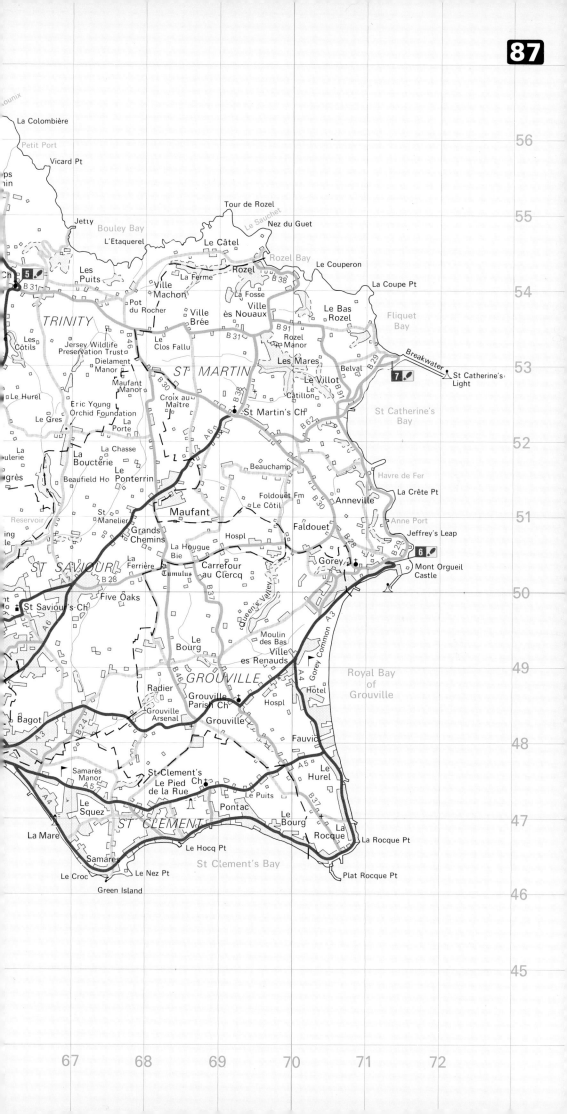

La Colombière

Petit Port

Vicard Pt

ps
nin

Jetty
Bouley Bay
Tour de Rozel
Le Sauchet
Nez du Guet

L'Etaquerel
Le Câtel
Rozel Bay
Le Couperon

Ch
5
Les
Puits
La Ferme
Rozel
B 38
La Coupe Pt

B 31
Ville
Machon
La Fosse
Ville
ès Nouaux
Le Bas
Rozel
Fliquet
Bay

Pot
du Rocher
Ville
Brée
B 91

TRINITY
Le
Clos Fallu
Rozel
Manor
Les Mares
Belval
B 29
Breakwater
St Catherine's
Light

Les
Côtils
Jersey Wildlife
Preservation Trust
B 46
ST MARTIN
Le Villot
7

Le Hurel
Dielament
Manor
Croix au
Maître
B 31
Le
Câtillon
B 91

Eric Young
Orchid Foundation
Maufant
Manor
B 30
St Martin's Ch
B 62
St Catherine's
Bay

Le Grès
La
Porte
A 6

La
ulerie
La Chasse
Beauchamp
Havre de Fer
La Crête Pt

grès
Beaufield Ho
La Boucterie
Le
Ponterrin
Foldouët Fm
Le Côtil
B 30
Anneville

Reservoir
St
Manelier
Maufant
Faldouet
Anne Port
Jeffrey's Leap

ing
le
Grands
Chemins
Hospl
B 28

ST SAVIOUR
La Hougue
Bie
6

A 7
B 28
La
Ferrière
Carrefour
au Clercq
Gorey
Mont Orgueil
Castle

Tumulus

Five Oaks
B 37

o
St Saviour's Ch
A 6
Le
Bourg
Queen's Valley
Moulin
des Bas
Gorey Common A 3

Ville
es Renauds
A 4
Royal Bay
of
Grouville

GROUVILLE
Hotel

Radier
Grouville
Parish Ch
Hospl

Bagot
B 24
Grouville
Arsenal
Grouville

Fauvic

A 5
Le
Hurel

Samarés
Manor
A 5
St Clement's
Ch
Le Pied
de la Rue
Le Puits
B 37

Le Squez
Pontac
Le
Bourg
La
Rocque

La Mare
ST CLEMENT
La Rocque Pt

A 4
Samarés
Le Hocq Pt

Le Croc
Le Nez Pt
St Clement's Bay
Plat Rocque Pt

Green Island

56
55
54
53
52
51
50
49
48
47
46
45

67   68   69   70   71   72

GUERNSEY

Côbo Bay

Côbo

Albecq

CAST

Vazon
Bay

Richmond

Le Gelé

Vazon

La
Porte

Lihou Island

Le Trepied

Perelle
Bay

Le
Marais

Rocque
Claire
Mare

Les Rouvets
Tropical
Gardens

St
Saviour

Mont Saint

Tomato
Museum

King's Mills

Les
Grantez

L'Erée

Les Crèux
ès Faies

Les Adams

Saviour
Resr

9

Frie
Baton

Les
Lohiers

La
Saline

Les Clos
Landais

Neuf
Chemin

Rocquaine
Bay

ST PIERRE
DU BOIS

ST
SAVIOUR

Les
Buttes

Le Douit

Le Catillion

Les
Islets

Le
Gron

Fort Grey
Maritime Museum

The Strawberry
Farm

Guernsey Zoo

Vi

The
Fairy Ring

Les Pezeries

L'es
Clercs

Les Sages

Les
Buttes

Airport

Guernsey Gold
and Silversmiths

The German
Occupation Museum

Pleinmont

TORTEVAL (de)

Les
Fontaines

Les
Falles

Les
Nouettes

La
Planque

La Pointe de
Pleinmont

Hougue
Anthan

TORTEVAL

Le
Planel

Les Martins

La
Villiaze

Les
Landes

Les
Houa

FOREST

8

Baie
de la Forge

Belle
Elizabeth

Les Laurens

La
Corbière

Pointe de la Moye

23   24   25   26   27   28   29

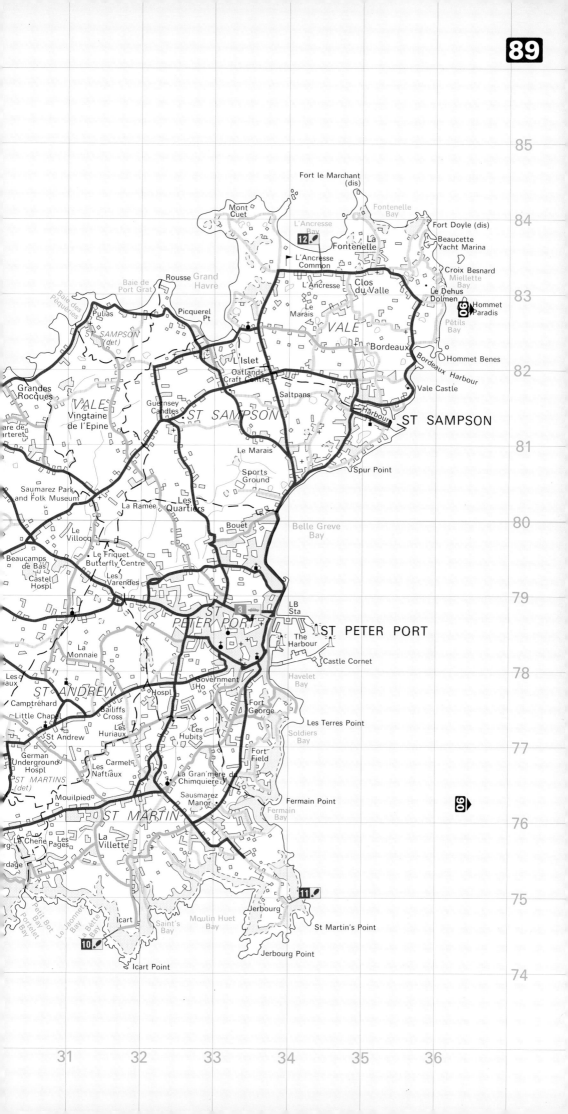

85

84

83

82

81

80

79

78

77

76

75

74

Fort le Marchant
(dis)

Fontenelle
Bay

Mont
Cuet

Fort Doyle (dis)

L'Ancresse
Bay

12

Beaucette
Yacht Marina

La
Fontenelle

Croix Besnard

L'Ancresse
Common

Miellette
Bay

Rousse Grand
Havre

L'Ancresse

Clos
du Valle

Le Dehus
Dolmen

09 Hommet
Paradis

Baie de
Port Grat

Le
Marais

Pètils
Bay

Picquerel
Pt

VALE

Baie des
Péqueries

Pulias

Bordeaux

Hommet Benes

ST SAMPSON
(det)

Bordeaux Harbour

L'Islet

Oatlands
Craft Centre

Vale Castle

Grandes
Rocques

Saltpans

Harbour

ST SAMPSON

VALE

Vingtaine
de l'Epine

Guernsey
Candies

ST SAMPSON

are de
arteret

Le Marais

Saumarez Park
and Folk Museum

Sports
Ground

Spur Point

La Ramée

Les
Quartiers

Bouet

Belle Greve
Bay

Le
Villocq

Beaucamps
de Bas

Le Friquet
Butterfly Centre

Les
Varendes

Castel
Hospl

LB
Sta

3

*ST
PETER PORT*

ST PETER PORT

La
Monnaie

The
Harbour

Castle Cornet

Les
iaux

ST ANDREW

Governement
Ho

Havelet
Bay

Camptrehard

Hospl

Little Chapel

Bailiffs
Cross

Fort
George

Les Terres Point

Les
Huriaux

Les
Hubits

Soldiers
Bay

St Andrew

German
Underground
Hospl

Les Carmel

Fort
Field

ST MARTINS
(det)

Les
Naftiaux

La Gran'mere du
Chimquiere

09 ▶

Mouilpied

Sausmarez
Manor

Fermain Point

Fermain
Bay

ST MARTIN

Le Chene

Les
Pages

La
Villette

rg

rdage

11

Jerbourg

Petit Bot
Bay

Le Jaonnet Bay

La Bette Bay

Icart

Saint's
Bay

Moulin Huet
Bay

St Martin's Point

10

Icart Point

Jerbourg Point

31   32   33   34   35   36

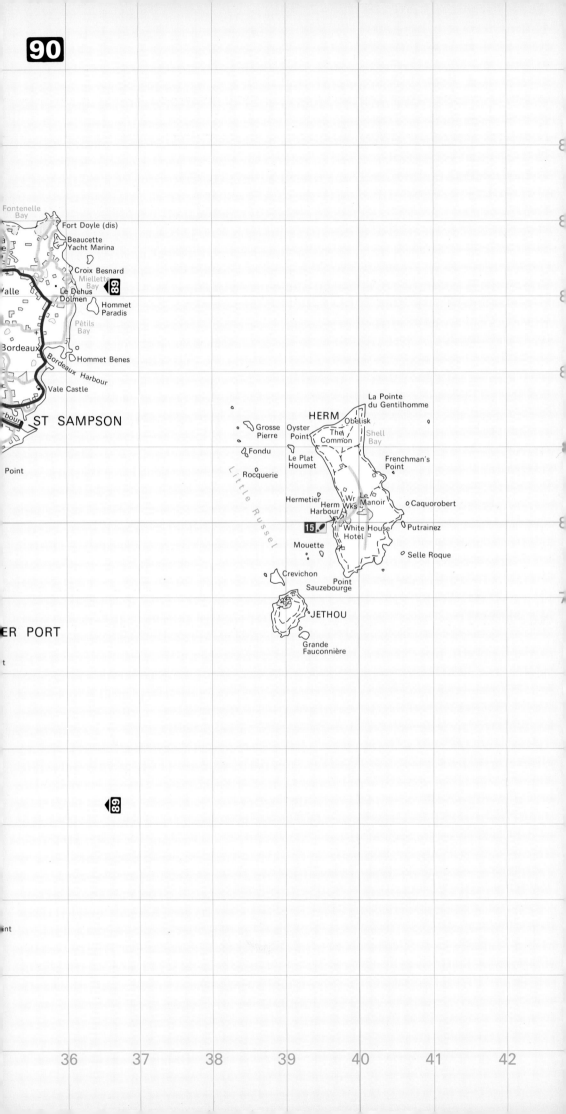

Fontenelle
Bay

Fort Doyle (dis)

Beaucette
Yacht Marina

Croix Besnard

Miellette
Bay

Le Dehus
Dolmen

Hommet
Paradis

Pêtils
Bay

Bordeaux

Hommet Benes

Bordeaux Harbour

Vale Castle

ST SAMPSON

Point

ER PORT

Grosse
Pierre

Fondu

Rocquerie

La Pointe
du Gentilhomme

HERM

Obelisk

Oyster
Point

The
Common

Shell
Bay

Le Plat
Houmet

Frenchman's
Point

Hermetier

Wr

Le
Manoir

Caquorobert

Herm Wks
Harbour

15

White House
Hotel

Putrainez

Mouette

Selle Roque

Crevichon

Point
Sauzebourge

JETHOU

Grande
Fauconnière

Little Russel

36   37   38   39   40   41   42

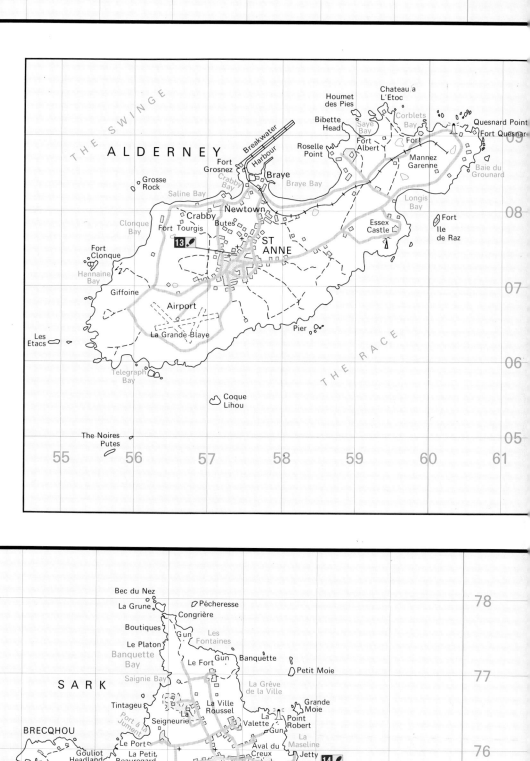

THE SWINGE

Houmet
des Pies
Chateau a
L'Etoc
Bibette
Head
Saye
Bay
Corblets
Bay
Quesnard Point
Fort Quesnar
Fort
Albert
Fort
Roselle
Point
Mannez
Garenne
Baie du
Grounard
ALDERNEY
Fort
Grosnez
Breakwater
Harbour
Braye
Braye Bay
Grosse
Rock
Saline Bay
Crabby
Bay
Newtown
Longis
Bay
Clonque
Bay
Crabby
Fort Tourgis
Butes
13
ST
ANNE
Essex
Castle
Fort
Ile
de Raz
Fort
Clonque
Hannaine
Bay
Giffoine
Airport
Les
Etacs
La Grande Blaye
Pier
THE RACE
Telegraph
Bay
Coque
Lihou
The Noires
Putes

05 06 07 08 03

55 56 57 58 59 60 61

Bec du Nez
La Grune
Pécheresse
78
Congrière
Boutiques
Gun
Les
Fontaines
Le Platon
Banquette
Bay
Le Fort
Gun
Banquette
Petit Moie
77
Saignie Bay
La Grève
de la Ville
SARK
Tintageu
La
La Ville
Roussel
Grande
Moie
BRECQHOU
Port à
Jument
Seigneurie
La
Valette
Point
Robert
Gun
Le Port
La
Maseline
76
Gouliot
Headland
La Petit
Beauregard
Aval du
Creux
Jetty
14
Havre
Gosselin
La Forge
Creux
Harbour
Les Burons
Les Dents
Mon
Gun
Moie des Orgeries
Derrible
Headland
Plaisance
75
La Grande
Grève
Point
Château
Derrible
Point
La Pointe de la Joue
Coupée
Baleine
Bay
LITTLE SARK
Baleine
74
Moie de la
Bretagne
La
Donnellerie
Mine
Chimneys
Sercul
Bretagne
Uset
Moie de Breniere
44 45 46 47 48 49
L'Etac

TOUR 1 27½ MILES
Around St Ouen's Bay

The route follows the flat coast road then winds uphill, allowing a magnificent view of La Corbière lighthouse. There are good views of the bay, which is the longest in the Channel Islands.

The drive starts from St Helier (see page 34). *From the Weighbridge, follow signs to the West, St Aubin A1 to leave by the Esplanade. In ½ mile at the traffic signals, go forward into Victoria Avenue A2. Just under two miles farther, bear left on to the A1 to reach Beaumont. At the mini-roundabout go forward (signed St Aubin).*

About ¾ mile further, reach St Aubin (see page 40). St Aubin's Bay has a beautiful sandy beach facing south.

Turn right onto the A13 (signed St Brelade, Corbière) and ascend St Aubin's Hill. In just over one mile, branch left onto the B66 (signed St Brelade's Church and Bay) and descend to St Brelade's Bay (see page 40). The bay has a sandy beach with rocks at the end. At the side of the 11th-century St Brelade's Church is the Fishermen's Chapel, parts of which date from the 6th century. The walls have paintings.

At the far end of the Bay by St Brelade's Church (on the left) turn left onto an unclassified road then at the T-junction turn right (signed Beau Port Bay) and ascend. The road has hairpin bends. After a short distance, pass the road to Beau Port Bay Car Park (on the left), then in ½ mile at the T-junction turn left into the B83 Route du Sud to reach La Corbière Lighthouse (on the left). La Corbière is a reef of jagged rocks on which stands the 62ft-high lighthouse. It is not open to the public but the lower gallery can be reached by a causeway at low tide. This is dangerous when the tide rises and a bell is rung to warn visitors to leave.

Continue with the B44, passing Petit Port Bay, then in ¾ mile turn left onto the B35 (signed La Pulente, St Ouen's Bay) and descend to La Pulente. Proceed along St Ouen's Bay (see page 40). St Ouen's Bay is the largest beach in the Channel Islands. It is most impressive and used for surfing, although due to the powerful undertow only experienced swimmers should bathe here. Above the sand dunes of Les Quennevais is an 18-hole golf course.

In 1½ miles, an AA telephone is passed on the right. In 1¼ miles, pass La Mielle de Morville Country Park and Nature Reserve on the right (see page 22), then in ¼ mile bear right (signed L'Étacq, St Ouen). After ½ mile, pass a quarry and turn sharp left (signed L'Étacq) to reach L'Étacq (see page 79). This is the northern extremity of St Ouen's Bay. From here to the ruins of Gros Nez Castle, a distance of 1½ miles, cliffs rise vertically to nearly 250ft. The workshops of L'Étacq Woodcraft are open to the public, as is the Potter's Wheel nearby where pottery and leatherwork may be seen.

After one mile, L'Étacq Point is reached. Ascend the hill and at the top turn sharp left onto the B55 (signed Gros Nez, Plémont). In ¾ mile turn left onto an unclassified road (signed Grosnez). Grosnez Point (with car park) is reached (see page 38). The ruins of a 13th-century castle can be seen at the point.

Return to the T-junction and turn left into the B55 Route de Grosnez. In ¾ mile go straight over the crossroads (signed Léoville), passing the road to Plemont Candlecraft (on the left). After 1⅓ miles turn sharp left onto the B65 (signed Grève de Lecq) and descend into La Grève de Lecq (see page 37). La Grève de Lecq is a small bay of orange sand. The Grève de Lecq Army Barracks, recently renovated by the National Trust for Jersey, contain displays of militaria and old Jersey horse-drawn vehicles. It is open during the summer.

Continue with the B40, passing Grève de Lecq Army Barracks on the left. In just over one mile, go over the crossroads, then ⅓ mile further go forward on the B33 (signed St John). An AA telephone is passed on the right. Go straight on for 1¾ miles to St John's Church. Go straight over the crossroads and turn immediately right onto the A10 (signed St Lawrence, St Helier) to reach Le Carrefour Selous, and go straight over the crossroads. In one mile, pass St Lawrence's Church (on the right). In 1⅓ miles at the T-junction, turn left onto the A1 (signed St Helier). In 1¼ miles at the roundabout take the second exit then go forward at the traffic signals. Proceed along the Esplanade to re-enter St Helier.

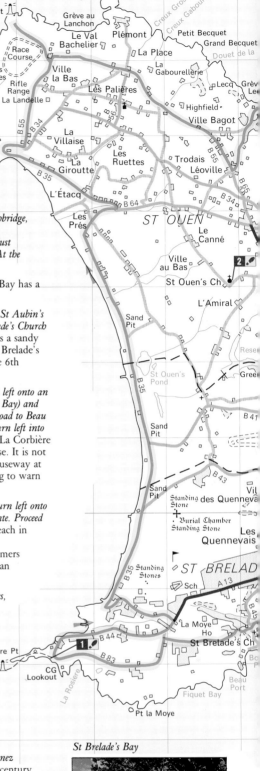

St Brelade's Bay

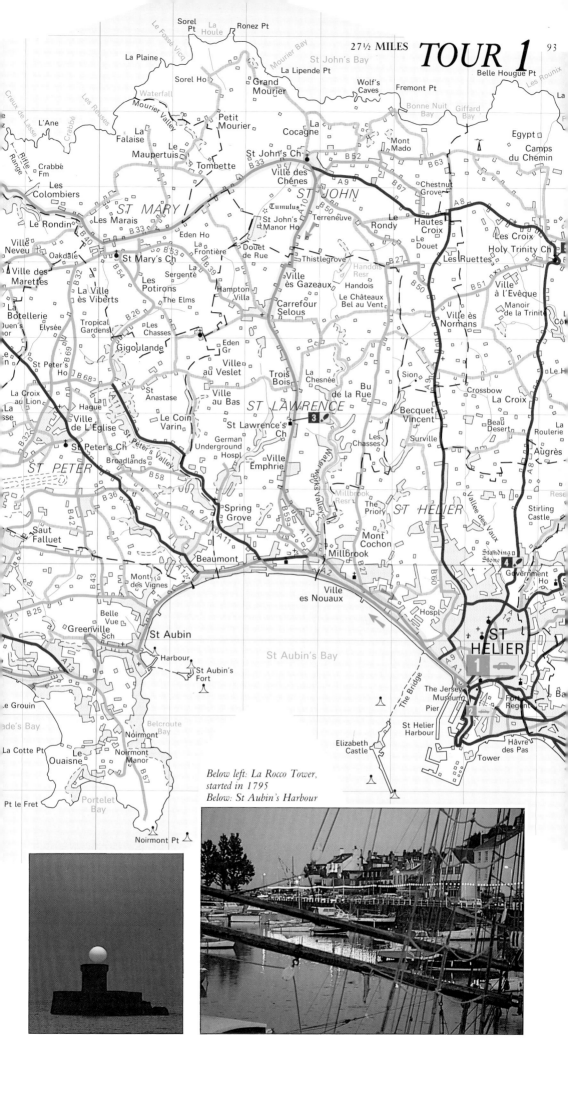

Below left: La Rocco Tower, started in 1795
Below: St Aubin's Harbour

TOUR 2
The North Jersey Coastline

25 MILES

When France was the enemy the picturesque northern beaches and bays of Jersey were part asset, part liability. Their quiet secretiveness, which enchants so many visitors today, made them vulnerable as hidden routes for stealthy invasion from the sea. It also made them ideal for stationing lookouts, who enjoyed an uninterrupted panorama of the French coast. Peace reigns, the castles are quiet and the views remain as wide as ever.

The drive starts from St Helier (see page 34), Jersey's thriving main town with a parish church dating from the 11th century. Islet-bound Elizabeth Castle – accessible by ferry, or on foot at low tide – was built in 1594. Remains of 19th-century Fort Regent have been converted into a leisure centre. Various interesting displays can be seen in the Jersey Museum.

From the Weighbridge in St Helier follow signs The West, St Aubin A1, leaving the town by The Esplanade. In ½ mile at traffic signals drive forward into Victoria Avenue, A2. In nearly ¾ mile turn right (signed Waterworks Valley A1). Continue to crossroads, at which go forward on the B27 signed Mont Cochon. In nearly three miles at the T-junction turn left onto an unclassified road, then turn right. After a further ½ mile at crossroads turn right, then at fork bear left. In ½ mile at T-junction turn right to follow the A9 to Les Haute Croix.

At T-junction turn left onto the A8, signed Trinity Church, Bouley Bay, then immediately turn right. In almost a mile take the second turning left, C96 signed Bouley Bay, and in nearly ½ mile at T-junction bear left and descend through sharp bends to Bouley Bay (see page 42). Excellent underwater swimming can be enjoyed from the bay's steep sand beach.

Return from the bay and ascend through sharp bends, with views of the French coast and Ecrebous Reefs. After nearly a mile take the first left turn onto the C95. Some ¾ mile farther continue forward, then at T-junction turn left onto the C93, signed Rozel Bay (see page 48). For beach keep left at foot of hill. This is a pleasant resort with a sand and rock beach, at the junction of two small valleys.

Continuing, bear right onto the B38 and climb. In a mile turn left onto the B91, signed Flicquet, St Catherine's, and in ½ mile at crossroads go forward onto an unclassified road (not for large cars, which should turn right at crossroads for St Catherine's) signed Flicquet Bay. Descend a narrow, winding hill road to Flicquet Bay.

Ascend, and just after ½ mile at T-junction turn left onto the B91. After another ½ mile at crossroads turn left onto the B29 (signed St Catherine). Continue round a one-way system for St Catherine's Breakwater (see page 49) and a return to the crossroads. The breakwater was built by the British Government in the mid-19th century as a response to French coastal fortification. The arm extending from L'Archirondel is some 2300ft long. Work was abandoned because of design faults and the advent of steamships.

On rejoining the crossroads after the one-way system turn left (signed Anne Port, Gorey). In just over a mile reach L'Archirondel. In just over ½ mile pass Anne Port and then Mont Orgueil Castle, then at T-junction turn sharp left (signed Gorey Harbour, St Helier A3). At the harbour keep right on the A3 (signed St Helier), and in ½ mile pass on the right a road for Gorey Village and on the left the Royal Jersey Golf Course. Mont Orgueil Castle is a formidable 13th-century and later fortress that towers over the port (see page 46) and its tiny harbour from a rocky summit some 310ft above sea level. Open to the public in summer, it affords magnificent views. The Jersey Pottery, in the village, can also be visited.

After passing the golf course, pass an AA telephone box on the right. Pass Grouville Post Office and keep left on the A4, signed La Rocque, St Helier. After La Rocque Harbour (see page 47), in just over a mile, reach Le Hocq (Le Hocq Inn), then in just over two miles at a mini roundabout turn left, signed Mount Bingham. Pass a bathing pool to Mount Bingham. Turn left, then turn sharp right, passing the harbour to re-enter St Helier.

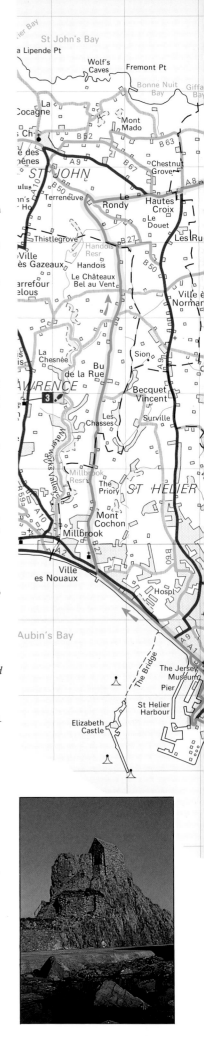

Right: The Hermitage at Elizabeth Castle
Opposite: La Rocque is a peaceful haven now, but a plaque recalls the French invasion of 1781

St Catherine's Bay and its half-mile breakwater

Les Rounix
Egue Pt
La Colombière
Petit Port
Egypt
Vicard Pt
Camps du Chêmin
Jetty
Bouley Bay
Le Sauchet
Tour de Rozel
Nez du Guet
s Croix
L'Etaquerel
Le Câtel
y Trinity Ch **5**
B 31
Les Puits
Ville Machon
La Ferme
Rozel
Rozel Bay
La Coupe Pt
B 38
lle l'Evêque
Pot du Rocher
Ville Brée
La Fosse
Ville ès Nouaux
Le Bas Rozel
Fliquet Bay
Manoir de la Trinité
TRINITY
Les Côtils
Le Clos Fallu
B 31
Rozel Manor
B 91
Belval
B 29
7
Breakwater
Jersey Wildlife Preservation Trust
Dielament Manor
ST MARTIN
B 30
Les Mares
Le Villot
Le Câtillon
St Catherine's Light
Le Hurel
Maufant Manor
Croix au Maître
B 38
St Martin's Ch
St Catherine's Bay
Le Gres
Eric Young Orchid Foundation
La Porte
B 46
Havre de Fer
Croix
La Roulerie
La Chasse
La Boucterie
Le Ponterrin
Beaufield Ho
Beauchamp
Foldouët Fm
Le Côtil
B 30
Anneville
La Crête Pt
Augrès
A 8
Reservoir
St Manelier
Maufant
Faldouet
Anne Port
Jeffrey's Leap
Stirling Castle
Grands Chemins
La Ferrière
Hospl
La Hougue Bie
Gorey
6
Mont Orgueil Castle
ST SAVIOUR
A 7
B 28
Cumulus
Carrefour au Clercq
B 37
Queen's Valley
A 4
4
Government Ho
St Saviour's Ch
Five Oaks
A 6
Le Bourg
Moulin des Bas
Ville es Renauds
Gorey Common A 3
Royal Bay of Grouville
ER
B 46
GROUVILLE
Hotel
Radier
Grouville Parish Ch
Hospl
Fort Regent
A 3
Bagot
B 24
Grouville Arsenal
Grouville
A 4
Fauvic
Hâvre des Pas
Samarès Manor
St Clement's Ch
Le Pied de la Rue
Le Puits
Le Hurel
A 5
Le Squez
Pontac
Le Bourg
La Rocque
Le Croc
La Mare
Samarès
ST CLEMENT
Le Hocq Pt
La Rocque Pt
Le Nez Pt
St Clement's Bay
Plat Rocque Pt
Green Island

BATTLE OF JERSEY
JANUARY 6TH 1781
THE FRENCH TROOPS UNDER THE COMMAND
OF BARON DE RULLECOURT
CAME ASHORE HERE

TOUR 3 29½ MILES
Around the Guernsey Shore

After running north along Les Banques to the port and shopping centre of St Sampson, this round-the-island tour follows a coast road alongside pleasant bays and over picturesque cliffs, affording fine sea views. After the bay and fort at Rocquaine the route switches between coastal and inland ways until it finally cuts across country and returns to St Peter Port.

The drive starts from St Peter Port (see page 50), Guernsey's hillside and harbour town with cobbled streets and steep steps, dominated by the stern military presence of ancient Castle Cornet. The stronghold now houses a museum of militaria. Above the town markets is Hauteville House, the exile home of eccentric French writer Victor Hugo, which is maintained in its original state and can be visited.

From the Weighbridge in St Peter Port follow the coast north for just over 2½ miles to St Sampson (see page 58), then at a mini-roundabout turn right. Continue for a mile to Bordeaux Harbour (see page 59), and at the T-junction at the end of the harbour turn right. Follow the main road, passing on the right the road to Debus Dolmen Ancient Monument and then the L'Ancresse Golf Course – also on the right – and an AA telephone box on the left. Dehus Dolmen is a particularly fine prehistoric burial chamber with good carvings and a passageway with side chambers – all lit.

Continue, then almost immediately at crossroads turn right (signed Bay, Car Park). Follow the coast road in a circular route and in almost a mile at T-junction turn left. In about ¾ mile arrive back at crossroads and turn right to rejoin the main road to reach Vale Church and turn right (signed West Coast). In ¼ mile bear left, then shortly right. In about ½ mile at L'Islet crossroads turn right and follow the coast road about 2½ miles to Grandes Rocques, then after ½ mile Cobo (see page 60). Cobo has a sandy beach with rocky pools that are ideal for observing marine life.

In just over another mile reach Vazon Bay (see page 62). Dominated by Fort Hommet, the beach here can be dangerous but is popular with surfers, and is used for sand racing.

Leave Vazon Bay and in nearly two miles pass Perelle Garage – and the road to Les Rouvets Tropical Vinery and Gardens – on the left and keep right. Continue to Fort Saumarez and bear left to follow the coast road. After just over 1¼ miles reach Rocquaine Bay (see page 66) and Fort Grey. The bay has a sand and rock beach and Fort Grey, which was originally built to keep French invaders at bay, has been restored to house a maritime museum with particular emphasis on shipwrecks around the Guernsey coast.

Top: Grandes Rocques, haunt of sunbathers
Above: Working boats at Bordeaux, a naturally formed harbour

After ½ mile at the Imperial Hotel turn left (signed St Peter Port), and ascend. At the top of the climb (where a path leads off right to the cliffs), turn left with the major road. In 1¼ miles pass Torteval Church on the left, and in another ½ mile bear right then keep to the main road. At Forest Road crossroads turn right to pass the Airport, then bear left – passing a road to the German Occupation Museum on the right. The museum claims to hold the largest collection of authentic German Occupation relics in the Channel Islands.

A beautiful bay, and a timely caution

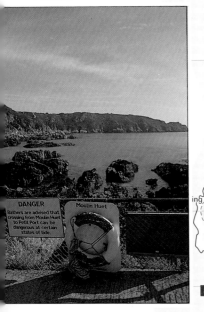

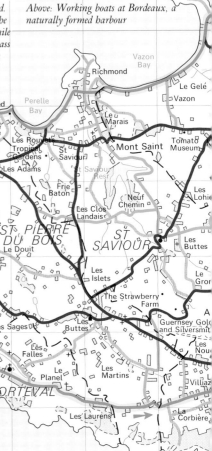

After passing the road to the museum on the right, immediately turn sharp right, signed Petit Bot Bay, and descend to Petit Bot Bay. Pleasant coastal scenery complements a sand and rock beach, overlooked by a reinforced Martello tower.

Ascend from the bay and take the first turning sharp right. After ½ mile at T-junction turn right, then immediately bear right. At the next T-junction turn right, and in nearly ½ mile at another T-junction turn right again, signed Icart. Continue to Icart car park. Icart Point, a promontory joined to the headland by a narrow ledge, is known as Chateau d'Icart and separates Petit Bôt from Saints Bay – so called from two rocks known as The Saints.

Return from the car park to the main road and keep forward. In ¼ mile at T-junction turn right and immediately left. In ¾ mile at crossroads turn left, then at T-junction turn right. After another ¼ mile at traffic signals go forward (signed Jerbourg) to reach Jerbourg car park, then return to traffic signals and turn sharp right, signed St Peter Port. In just over a mile bear right and descend. Re-enter St Peter Port by Le Val des Terres.

Right: Beaucette Marina, an inspired use of an old quarry

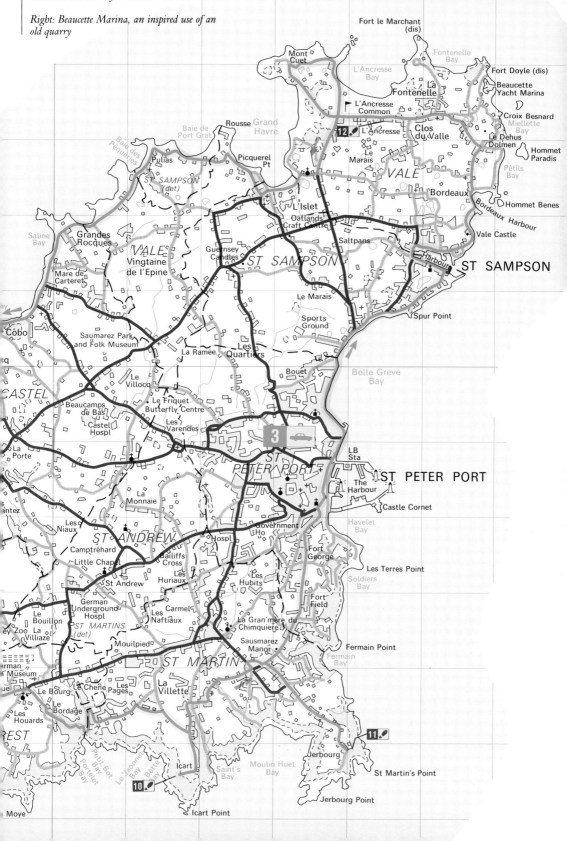

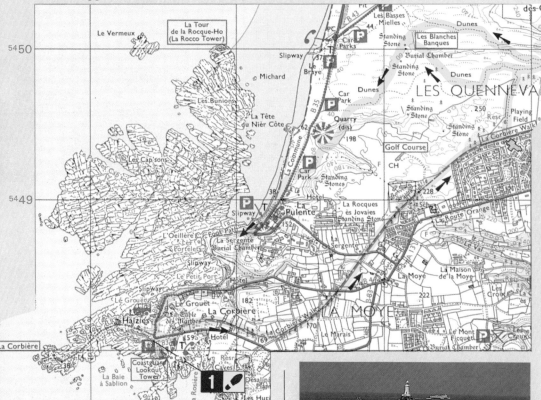

Western Dunes

Allow 3 hours   **JERSEY**

Apart from two short climbs towards the end of this walk, it is not strenuous. Botanists will particularly enjoy the dunes. The route of this walk crosses private and main roads, and walkers – particularly with young children – should take care.

Park in the car park to the right of the old railway station above La Corbière (WV554481). There is a convenient No 12 bus stop and a phone box. Walk on to the old railway line which runs parallel to the road and turn right. Immediately you will see La Table des Marthes, a large slab of red granite thought to be a capstone from a megalithic structure. Any contracts signed on this stone before 1850 were held to be binding. This could explain its name, or it could refer to a game played on its flat surface.

On the right is the tower of the desalination plant, used only during an acute water shortage. As the track crosses two roads the path becomes shady with evergreen oaks, chestnuts, sycamores and poplars arching the track, which passes La Moye Golf Club on the left.

Take the next turn left, off the main track, opposite Les Quennevais Secondary School. On the right are playing fields and on the left the golf course and then a pumping station. After an avenue of trees there is access on to the dunes to your left. Go through there and you are now on Les Blanches Banques. This is one of the most important dune systems in Europe, and is particularly rich in plant life. Creamy-white burnet roses fill the air with their scent in June and Jersey thrift, dwarf pansies and rare orchids are among more than 400 species to be found here, as well as several varieties of grass.

La Corbière Lighthouse

Keeping the magnificent view of St Ouen's Bay in front of you, make your way down any of the many paths to the foot of the dunes. As you reach the lower sandhills look out to sea. If La Rocco Tower, the round tower situated on rocks to the south of the bay, is on your left, you should be able to see a standing stone beneath you on the sandy plain. Head for that. When there, note the burial chamber (the ossuary) and its sister stone to the south. The worship of standing stones (menhirs) may have been one of the most primitive forms of religion.

Now keep walking south, towards La Corbière. The routes goes past a car park and up some steps, with a German bunker on the right. After the next car park, cross La Grande Route des Mielles (Five Mile Road) on to the footpath, still heading towards the lighthouse. On the right is the sea, and nearer to hand, abundant plant-life including wild fennel and sea stock.

Stay on this side of the road, past a drinking trough (abreuvoir) dated 1871, until the bend in the road. There is now a footpath leading round the cliff. Take the path up the cliff, which is private but a permitted footpath, to the top. Take a short detour here by turning left, and then right, for La Sergenté, the oldest tomb in Jersey, built around 3700BC.

Return to the top of the steps and take the path through zig-zag gates opposite. At the bottom turn left along a bridle path, left again and then right on to the road. This leads round to La Corbière past a German bunker, open to the public on Saturdays, and so back to the starting point.

Reservoir Ramble

Allow 3 hours   **JERSEY**

An energetic but beautiful walk around La Val de la Mare Reservoir and Les Mielles Country Park, with a tremendous variety of scenery. The path can be wet in places.

Park in the car park behind St Ouen's Parish Church (WV579530). St Ouen was a 7th-century archbishop of Rouen and the church was probably founded by an early member of the de Carteret family. It dates from before the 11th century.

In front of the church turn right and then first left (La Rue de la Campagne). On both sides of the road are strips of land separated by grass banks. These are fields still farmed in the medieval strip manner. *At the T-junction turn right and then left on to a track marked La Val de la Mare Reservoir. Take the left hand fork, and by a small parking area, go through the gate to the left.* Below is one arm of the Y-shaped Val de la Mare Reservoir, created in the early 1960s.

Follow the path down to the water, then north up the western arm, across a gravel causeway, up the hill between the two arms (with fantastic views and seats at the summit) and so down to the tip of the eastern arm, around and south down its length to the dam. This is 535ft along the crest and 75ft high from the valley floor, and contains 52,000 cubic yards of concrete.

Take the path down to the foot of the dam, and out to the road then turn right. Part of the route just taken followed the track of a German railway from the granite quarries at St John to La Pulente. This was never opened, but before turning on to La Rue De la Mare notice the concrete bridge crossing the road on the left. Sunset Nurseries, which is open to the public, is on the left. In the distance can be seen La Mare au Seigneur (St Ouen's Pond).

After the junction with Mont Matthieu and an area of sand-removal, turn right up a track, and when it forks bear left. The area soon becomes wooded and the path narrow. This section of the walk is known as Les Hanières after the Jersey-French *Han* meaning galingale which grows here. The path, which is often overgrown and can be extremely wet, leads to a farm, La Ville au Bas.

Turn left past the farm, along a ridge giving more panoramic views of the bay below and then take the second track to the left, marked as a footpath only (not the first steep path as this leads straight down!). This leads into another valley, Les Vaux Cuissin, with a babbling brook and a copse of recently planted hazel, white poplar, oak and elm. Finally, climb out on to Les Chemins des Monts.

Turn left into the road, and about 400yd on the left is a Neolithic passage grave. The Dolmen des Monts, Grantez, is a bottle-shaped grave, about 5ft below the present ground level. It was originally covered by a circular mound, and was virtually undisturbed when investigated in 1912. Eight skeletons were found inside, dating back some 5000 years.

After leaving the dolmen, cross the road on to a track. Keep bearing right into La Rue de Grantez. Ahead is St Ouen's Mill. This is now a shipping marker and the headquarters of a Scout Group. There has been a mill here since the 14th century and medieval strip fields can be seen around it.

Turn left at the next junction to get back to the church.

Val de la Mare Reservoir

WALK 3
Rural
St Lawrence

Allow 2 hours or 1½ hours **JERSEY**

This is a pretty walk, showing the best of this lush parish with its brooks, reservoirs and National Trust properties. Much of the route is on metalled roads, but some of the tracks can be overgrown.

Park in Rue de l'Eglise alongside the church (WV626518). The St Lawrence Pillar, standing inside the church, was found below the floor during restoration work in 1890 and proves that there was a church here at the beginning of the 7th century. It also has the oldest bell in Jersey (1592) and an unusual Norman saddle-back tower. Note the contained setting of this little community with the church, school, arsenal and parish hall all in a straight line, and the public house and shop just across the road.

Turn left on to main road and then right opposite the parish hall down a metalled track marked 'no road'. This soon becomes rough and steep and leads down into La Vallée de St Laurens (Waterworks Valley). Three reservoirs have been built in this valley over the last hundred years, but at one time the stream powered six or seven mills.

Those who are taking the shorter walk will turn left

Le Rât Cottage

on to the road at the bottom and should skip the next section until the more energetic return to this point. The others will turn right. The road winds through the valley to Millbrook reservoir. On the right the abreuvoir provided water for the horses carrying granite to build the St Aubin's sea wall at the turn of the century. The reservoir was the first to be built in the valley, in 1898, to provide water for St Helier. (The Jersey Fresh Water Angling Association have fishing rights here, but the public can stroll around it.)

Turn left, up Ruelle de St Clair, turning from time to time to admire the view. At the top of the road, turn left down a grass track between two private drives. This follows the course of a stream down into the valley again. At the bottom is the site of the mill pond of Moulin à Sucre, a mill which once crushed sugar. On the right various paths lead past the site of Vicart Mill and back to the original junction.

Turn right up the road, picking up those who chose the shorter walk, past Dannemarche Reservoir, built in 1909 and left up Mont de la Chenaie. At the top, turn left, then right on to the main road and immediately left again into Rue Milbrae. Keep straight on at next cross roads, down road marked 'no entry'. At the bottom of the hill are several National Trust for Jersey properties. On the left are two wooded côtils (steep fields) while on the right is Le Rât Cottage, a delightful 17th-century dwelling. Just past the junction to this cottage is La Fontaine de St Martin, an ancient sacred spring said to have healing powers. Just beyond, on the right, is an unusual abreuvoir, with the stream running on to the road and back. This was built as a lavoir (washing place) in the 17th century. Keep straight up the road to reach Morel Farm (NT) which has probably the most perfectly proportioned double roadside arch in the island, dated 1666, and interesting outbuildings. This is a working farm and the tenant cannot always show people round.

Turn left into Les Charrières de Malorey and when the road curves to the right, keep straight on into Le Chemin des Montagnes. Then turn left past Badier Farm. This is marked private but there is a public right-of-way leading straight past the house and on to a track. This leads down into a valley and then curves to the right. It eventually comes out on to the road behind the church.

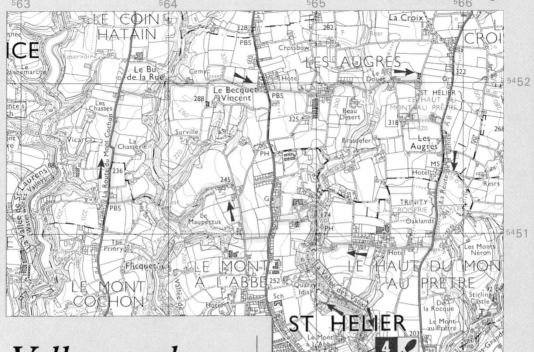

Valleys and Farms

Allow 2 hours **JERSEY**

This is an easy rural walk, close to St Helier. It follows country lanes winding up and down between the valleys leading into town, each with their cluster of working farms.

Park at a convenient spot about ¼ mile along Vallée des Vaux near the water garden (WV654503). The stream now meandering through the garden once worked a water mill at Town Mills, which served St Helier. On the other side of the road is Le Don Le Gallais. Don means 'gift of' and this was the first property to be given to the National Trust for Jersey.

Walk up the valley with the stream on your right. The road leads past La Pouquelaye steps (leading to Queen's Road) and Les Déserts (NT), which has an arboretum of unusual trees. Across the road is La Commune des Melèches – a gorse-covered slope of common land.

The route follows the road past the Harvest Barn Inn and yet more National Trust land. Take the first left up Rue des Côtils (very steep), which leads to the main road. Turn left on to Queen's Road, and then first right down a narrow lane. Turn right at the bottom past Fernhill. This 17th-century house, originally called L'Ancienne Maison Le Geyt, was the home of one Philippe Le Geyt, a lawyer of renown born in 1635.

Turn left and into Fern Valley. The narrow lane leads past a lovely old farm and into an aptly named valley. Not a mile from St Helier, the view is totally unspoilt.

When the junction with La Route du Mont Cochon is reached, turn right and walk along the road, turning right down the next public road, Ruette Pinel. Before turning east, note the view west, over La Vallée de St Laurence (Waterworks Valley), to St Lawrence Parish Church with its unusual tower. La Ruette Pinel leads back into the valley, past another farm

Dark-eyed, scallop-nosed Jersey cattle

and eventually up to Surville cemetery.

Cross the main road and follow the strawberry signs (during the picking season) along Rue du Becquet Vincent. This eventually descends to the top of Valley des Vaux, which means 'Valley of the Small Vales'. Past Le Douet Farm (Douet meaning a stream) turn left past Lyndale and then right at the T-junction. After another turn to the left, the reason for the strawberry signs becomes apparent. Fruit and vegetables can be picked at La Grange fruit farm.

Turn right on to Trinity main road (La Route de la Trinité). On the right can soon be seen the Sir Francis Cook Gallery, a converted chapel used by local artist Sir Francis Cook and given by his widow to the Jersey Heritage Trust in 1982. Different exhibitions are held here throughout the year. Past the Gallery and the Oaklands Lodge Hotel is Le Don Sparkes-Davies (NT). The Trust believes this curious, windowless building was erected to give its owner or occupier an influence or vote in the town parish.

Turn right into La Route du Petit Clos, which wends its way past another farm and so to the western slope of La Commune des Melèches. Some may wish to brave the gorse bushes of the common to reach the foot of the valley, but the road leads gently down to the entrance of the Harvest Barn. Turn left along the valley to your parking spot.

Cliff path at La Belle Hougue

Top of the Island

Allow 2½ hours **JERSEY**

A country and cliff-top walk which offers some of the most spectacular scenery in the island. It is steep at times, but along the coastal path there are seats at regular intervals. Binoculars would be an advantage for bird-watchers.

Park in Rue du Presbytère, east of Trinity Church (WV662540). The interior of this 11th-century church is plain, but note a fine 17th-century mural memorial against the north wall of the Lady Chapel to Sir Edouard de Carteret, Black Rod under Charles II.

Head north, past the Parish Hall on your right. Turn right at T-junction (signposted to Bouley Bay). The strip of land on the right belongs to the National Trust for Jersey, and is planted with hydrangeas, fuschias and other flowering shrubs.

Take the first turning left down a lane which bears left. Turn right down a narrow path to the left of a private drive to 'Fresh Springs'. This spot is called Le Puchot (a watercourse in the form of a pond). The stream runs through an enclosure containing a lavoir (to do the washing) and a well-head fronted by a wrought iron gate.

Follow path through zig-zag gates down through woods, past iris beds on left to main road. Turn left on

to road, and then *left again up one-way road. Turn right up next track opposite 'no entry' junction and follow the track round to the left.* Turn around for a superb view of the countryside. It is also possible to see remnants of a military guardhouse, on the right towards the top of the climb. At the summit are views of the French coastline and, to the right, the north coast of the island is a glorious tapestry of colour.

Continue along the westward path until faced with a wooded valley, a small cove and a fishing hut. The ruined houses to the left of the modern house on the facing hillside are the remains of Égypte (Egypt), a farm used by the Germans during the Occupation to practise street-to-street fighting.

At the junction in the woods turn right and down a steep incline. At the next junction take the right turn, marked Bonne Nuit. (A 100yd detour over the stream leads to another ruined cottage). The path now goes past the beach of Petit Port and Wolfs Lair, the fishing hut, and along an area where wild flowers are particularly prevalent. Next there is the headland of La Belle Hougue, and halfway to its summit, tucked away down a little path to the right, can be found La Fontaine ès Mittes, a mineral spring said to give speech to the dumb and to cure eye complaints. Nonetheless it is a little murky these days.

Another few yards up the slope there is a sign to the main road. If you are strong enough, ignore it and take the path to the right. At the summit of La Belle Hougue, Bonne Nuit Bay can be seen below.

Take the upper path. Below lies Le Havre Giffard (Giffard Bay), sometimes known as Dead Man's Bay as the protruding rock resembles a human body.

At the white sign forbidding motor-cycles, take minor path left, towards a bungalow. Turn right on to a track, and then left on to the metalled road. To the left is Les Platons, the highest point in the island, with the radio transmission masts.

Keep to the road until the junction at Le Vescont Monument (a granite obelisk commemorating a Trinity constable or mayor) and then take the first turning left. This road returns to the starting point.

Royal Bay

Allow 2½ hours or 1 hour **JERSEY**

Apart from the initial climb, this is an easy walk through country lanes, which offers marvellous views, a fair chunk of history and a chance to curl your toes in the sand on the final stretch.

Park on coast road near Gorey (Gouray) Pier or by Castle Green (WV714504). If below the castle, walk up footpath just round the corner from the pier to Castle Green. Turn left and, crossing the road, go up Mont de la Garenne, marked 'no entry'. At the seat half-way up, or at the top, take time to admire the view of Mont Orgueil Castle, the harbour and the great sweep of the Royal Bay of Grouville.

At the top, turn right (Rue des Marettes) and follow sign to dolmen, which is found through an avenue of trees on the left. This Neolithic grave was once probably covered by a mound. It has been altered since it was first discovered in the 17th century, but experts think it was a passage-grave with a horseshoe-shaped chamber, formed by seven uprights and covered by an enormous 24-ton capstone. The western end of the passage was probably dug out later to form a second grave. When first discovered, it was believed to be a Druid Temple – hence the name of the adjacent house, Temple View.

After making this detour, continue down Rue des Marettes in the same direction, turning left into La Grande Route de Faldouet, and then first right after the Garden Centre. Grassfort, the old house on the right, has the best example of a double round arch that has been altered. The arch over the pedestrian entrance has been replaced by a straight lintel engraved 17 CCL 25. Further down the road, on the same side, there is a double arch entrance with an early marriage stone over the pedestrian entrance dated 1740, with the initials CAB and AC separated by a heart.

About 300 yards down the road, turn left. Bear left at the next fork and then take the second turning right at 'no entry' sign. The road now leads past the prize-winning Gorey Village development, and the back entrance to the Jersey Pottery, the largest pottery in the Channel Islands, with more than 200 lines made and sold on the premises.

For those taking the short walk, it is now possible to cut through Gorey Village on to the coast road and back to the Pier. For the full walk, keep on the same road, walking south-west. On the left is Grouville Marsh – an important stretch of wetland which harbours a number of wintering wildfowl, including teal and common snipe. It is also a stop-over point for many migrating birds and is frequently used by Jersey's bird-ringers. Lower Mill Pottery is housed in one of three old mills that were once powered by the stream running through Queen's Valley.

Turn left into La Rigondaine, and left again to go past the parish church. Straight ahead at this junction is the road known as Blood Hill, named after a particularly violent medieval battle at the top of the hill, at a spot now known as La Croix de la Bataille. Grouville Church (St Martin of Grouville) has a long history. A memorial in the churchyard is dedicated to soldiers of the 83rd Regiment, killed at La Rocque on the day of the Battle of Jersey in 1781.

Continue past the church, take the second turn right past a tiny chapel and, crossing the Coast Road, take the road towards the Grouville Bay Hotel and the sea. Straight ahead is Fort Henry, a square-towered defence built during the governorship of Sir Henry Seymour Conway (1772-1795). The route leads past the Royal Jersey Golf Club, whence have come the golfers Harry Vardon, five-times winner of the British Open Championship, Ted Ray, who held both the British and American titles, Aubrey Boomer, five-times champion of France, and Tommy Horton.

Either head back towards the castle along the sea-wall (watching out for flying golf balls) or go along the beach. Either way, the last lap will be along the track of the old eastern railway, past colourful flower-beds and the memorial to Gorey shipbuilders. If parked at Castle Green, walk up the public gardens opposite this memorial for a pleasant and scented finale.

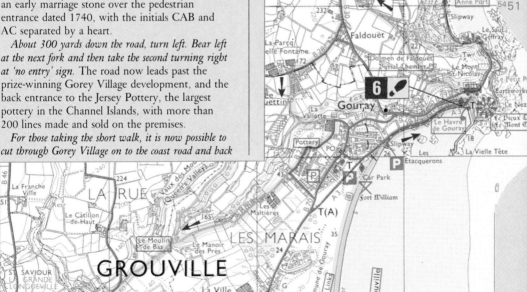

WALK 7
Secret
St Martin

Allow 2½ hours **JERSEY**

The beautiful Parish of St Martin is shown at its best on this walk which wanders along cliff paths, through woods, down Rozel Valley, past some lovely old houses and into the lesser-known inlets on the north-east coast. The woods can be muddy, so sensible shoes are advisable. This walk is for the sure-footed, as some of the paths are narrow with steep drops alongside.

Park at St Catherine's Breakwater (WV764530) and walk west along the road past St Catherine's Yacht Club. At the first cove take the little cliff path as far as the slipway and St Catherine's Tower. Then rejoin the road. Turn right at 'no entry' sign and then bear left. La Masseline Reservoir, built by the Germans during the last war and now popular with a local angling club for coarse and trout fishing, is on the right. Ahead are Rozel Woods, reached by crossing the stream twice by stepping stones (the path can be muddy). Red squirrels can often be seen here, and it is also a breeding place for the greater spotted woodpecker. This valley is also one of the few places in Jersey where yellow archangel, dog's mercury, climbing white fumitory and wood sorrel can be found. The stream on the right is always ablaze with flag irises in the spring. Ignore the first path to the left – this is where the sanctuary path from St Martin's Parish Church joins the one we have just taken.

Turn right at the bridge and go up a track known as Rue des Mares, which is shown on a 19th-century map to have once been a road. *Note the first glimpse of Rozel Manor (Le Manoir de Rosel) on the left. At the end of the path turn left on to road – La Chasse Fleurie. Keep to the road, which bears left, and then turn left again into La Grande Route de Rozel (marked to St Martin's Church).* Below, on the left, is another view of the manor.

Bear to the right and then turn first right (Rue du Moulin). On the left, set in private land, is Le Moulin de Rozel (Rozel Mill), one of the oldest windmills in Jersey, shown on Popinjay's map of 1563. Further down the valley, on the right, willows are still grown for basket-making, and further still, at the foot of the hill, an old fountain is set into the wall of a cottage. Turning right, the road passes an area planted out with many rare and beautiful trees, mostly the work of Samuel William Curtis, editor of the Botanical Magazine, who lived in this valley at the beginning of the 19th century.

At the next junction, the slip to Rozel Bay (La Havre de Rozel) is straight ahead, and the village to the left. However, turn to the right, admiring the view of the little harbour as you climb the hill. At the top, just past the Bistro Frère Restaurant, turn left down a track called Rue des Fontenelles. This path leads past steep, cultivated côtils, across a stream running into a secluded inlet, Douet de la Mer, and so to Le Havre de Scez (Saie Harbour). On the left is Le Couperon Dolmen, one of only two known gallery graves in Jersey. One of the stones at the eastern end of the cist, which has a cut-out semi-circle, was put in the wrong position during one of its restorations. Saie Harbour itself is notable for its strange pudding-mix rock formation.

La Coupe Point is straight ahead, but there is as yet no cliff path here, so take the road up the hill, and ignoring the first turning left, take the next – La Rue de la Perruque. This leads to Fliquet, another little-used bay with a defensive tower known as Telegraph Tower. Then take the cliff path back to St Catherine's Breakwater.

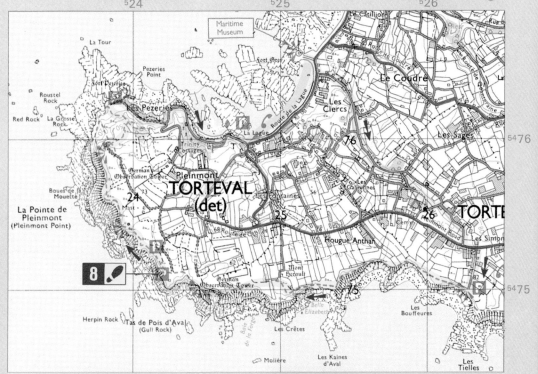

The Edge of the Ocean

Allow 2¼ hours   **GUERNSEY**

Below the cliff top at Pleinmont, fishing boats pick their way among rocks which other sailors go miles to avoid. There is nothing between here and America.

Park at Pleinmont (WV242753). Walk along the cliff path, with the sea on the left. This is one of the path's most dramatic sections. Offshore, the Hanois lighthouse was built in 1859, on the wicked granite reef that once took a steady toll of ships. The German watchtower is one of a chain which fixed targets by triangulation, made obsolete by radar. When the path takes a sharp right bend, look for a cube of concrete inscribed H 12 behind the seat. This was once a German minefield.

Cross the car park bearing left, and turn left where a sign stone indicates Cliff Path and Portelet, descending to another car park. On the way, the circular mound of the Table des Pions was a resting place for the 'Chevauchée de S Michel', an annual procession of the Court which examined the roads and sea defences. The Pions, handsome young footmen, could kiss any woman they met on the way.

Continue past Fort Pezeries along the coast road, going past little Portelet Harbour to Rocquaine Bay. You can walk along the sand at most states of the tide to Fort Grey, known locally as the 'Cup and Saucer', now a maritime museum.

Rejoin the coast road here, and walk back south for about 80 yards. Turn left by the cottage called Le Crocq du Sud. The road climbs gently up a sheltered valley. Take the fourth right turning, up a road towards the spire of Torteval Church. Turn left at the top into the

Fort Grey Maritime Museum

pathway and go over a car park and through the churchyard to the road. Turn left. The 1818 church replaced an older one, but has one of the original bells, cast in 1432.

In 100 yards turn right into a lane. Bear right at the first junction and follow to the main road. Turn left and, in 100 yards, turn right where a sign stone indicates Les Tielles. The walk leads to the sea and, given good eyes and a clear day, gives views to the lighthouse on the Plateau des Roches Douvres, 23 miles away and straight ahead.

Turn right on the cliff path (sign stone 'Pleinmont Pt'). After about a mile, near the watch house on a hill, the path joins a partly tarmac-surfaced track which eventually bends right round a field. At this point take the path again to the left, to go back to the starting point. The 1804 watch house was one of a chain which stood guard against Napoleon. Just before it note Belle Elizabeth and Petite Elizabeth – a conical rock at the foot of the cliff, with a smaller rock nearby. The story goes that Elizabeth, a beautiful local girl, had an illegitimate child and was banished from home by her indignant father. In despair, she threw herself from the cliff, her baby in her arms, and both were turned into the rocks you see.

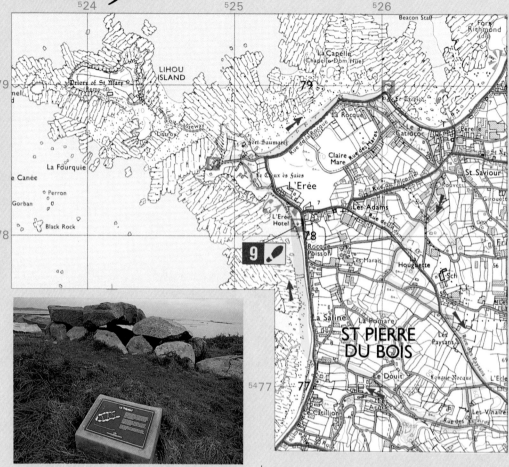

Le Trepied – a haunt of witches?

Witches and Fairies

Allow 1¾ hours   **GUERNSEY**

The entrance to fairyland and a notorious witchcraft site, Le Catioroc, are passed on the route, which is rich in prehistoric remains.

Park at L'Erée (WV254781). With the sea on the left, walk a short distance up the main road and take the left turning just past an old bunker, onto the headland of L'Erée. After a short distance, a sign points to the dolmen of Creux ès Faies, which is worth a visit. It was supposed to be an entrance to Fairyland.

The walk continues to the car park overlooking the strait to Libou Island. The ancient causeway was first built by the monks of the Priory of St Mary Libou, a 12th-century foundation and possibly the Church's answer to the witches at Le Catioroc. At the end of the car park, the 'Prosperity' memorial commemorates a disastrous shipwreck.

Return up the approach road and bear left at the fork below the German tower. Turn left on to the coast road, or walk over the shingle beach to the next slipway. The field on the other side of the road was the aerodrome from which Sir Alan Cobham pioneered air services to Bournemouth in 1937,

the journey taking two to three hours. Half a mile along the road, follow the sign pointing to an ancient monument and climb to Le Trépied dolmen, Le Catioroc. It is mentioned in the transcripts of many local witchcraft trials and there are eye-witness accounts of the Friday-night sabbaths. People avoided the place well into the 19th century.

The walk follows the path over an old gun position and through a pine wood, and becomes a macadamed lane. Cross over the main crossroads and turn right past the Tropical Gardens. At the top of the hill, double back on the right turning and, in 80 yards, turn left into a footpath. Coming to the main road, cross over to the footway, turn left and in a few yards turn right down a lane. At the next junction, turn left and, ignoring a left turning, keep going until you join the main Les Paysans Road (Rue des Paysans), bearing right to walk onwards up the hill. A large standing stone can be seen through a gateway on the right. This too is of pagan origin and, within living memory, Guy Fawkes night bonfires were lit here. The guy was called the Bout'lot (now 'Budloe'), a corruption of Bout de L'an – end of the year. The custom derives from pagan winter solstice ceremonies.

Take the next right turn at a staggered crossroads, then take the first left and, at the end of this road, turn right. In a wall on the left, a little way down, there is a stone inscribed 'James de Garis 1895'. He was a renowned carpenter and boat builder who made very fine fishing boats here and trundled them down to the sea along this lane.

Bear right at the first fork and left at the second. Keep going towards the sea, which can be seen occasionally. Reaching the coast, turn right to return to the starting point.

Dramatic Bays

Allow 2½ hours **GUERNSEY**

This walk follows the cliff path to the beautiful little fishing harbour at Saints Bay and on to Moulin Huet Bay before turning inland on quiet lanes to Petit Bôt. From this cliff-girt cove, the coastal path returns to Icart through a landscape of rocks and wild flowers.

Park at the viewpoint car park at the end of Icart road (WV317746). Turn left on to the cliff path following the sign stone to Saint's Bay. As the path rises sharply above Icart Point, it reveals a panorama which includes Moulin Huet Bay, Petit Port and, in the distance, Sark and Jersey.

At the highest point, the path bends left. Keep to the right just past a seat on the left. When the path bends left again, look out for the steps in front of the seat there and descend to Saint's Harbour. The cobbles on the slipway are angled to provide a hold for horses. The wall at the top of the beach was part of the island's defences against Napoleon. The bay is a favourite resort for summer visitors who, one morning in 1967, found a very large freighter stuck fast on the rocks.

Walk up the macadamed road past the Martello tower and, at the end, turn left up the hill. In a few paces, turn right between half barriers on a path where a sign stone indicates Moulin Huet and Petit Port. *Keep on along the coastal path.* Seats mark the best viewpoints, the first overlooking Saints Bay and another on the headland above the bay of Bon Port.

On reaching the road, go straight up it past the pottery to a little crossroads and double back left up the hill; the road bends right past Blanchlande College. Carry on to a right bend and keep straight forward at the junction which follows, past the Captain's Hotel, then turn left immediately afterwards and go straight over the crossroads. This is the Rue des Grons, where the ghostly howl of Tchico, legendary dog of death, was said to presage doom and disaster.

Walk on to a staggered crossroads and go straight over, leaving Le Clos des Fontaines to the right. Turn right at the end of the road and almost immediately left into a lane. Descending, on the left is an old house called La Falaise, whose owner had a feudal duty to look out for pirates and enemy ships. There is a collection of traditional Guernsey doorway arches in the grounds, made during the 19th century when they went out of fashion for a time.

Where the road bends sharply right just past the house, walk straight forward on the footpath which begins on the bend. Go down the steps, bear left where the path divides and climb the steps to the cliff top. There is a good view over the dramatic cove of Petit Bôt with the little bay of Portelet beyond. Notice the battery site and magazine on the far hillside.

Follow the cliff path one mile back to the starting point, keeping left at the junction with path to the bay of Le Jaonnet (meaning a furze brake) and also passing La Bette Bay.

Plants flourish in the southern shelter of Moulin Huet

WALK 11
Castle of
Refuge

Allow 2½ hours   **GUERNSEY**

A strenuous walk with steep stretches but worth the effort. It explores the last, rock-bound refuge of the islanders, from French raiders in the Middle Ages.

Park at Jerbourg Point (WV340749). From the car park, Jersey, Sark and the French coast can be seen. Take the steps of the cliff path, going down from the left seaward corner, and Jethou and Herm will appear, merged together from this angle, with Alderney as well on a clear day. During World War II, the squat Bréhon Tower in the channel mounted a German anti-aircraft battery which shot down two aircraft, one from each side. St Martin's Point comes into sight with a white, box-like lighthouse. Here the pirate Richard Higgins was

East-facing Fermain, a popular morning bay

hanged in 1565, and left to rot.

At the seat, take the steps leading off to the left. A little way down, turn left again, on a path which is marked with sign stones and goes towards Fermain Bay, one mile away. At a T-junction above the bay, turn right to pass some seats overlooking the sea. This is a pretty walk, with views up the east coast and over the sea to the other islands. Fermain Bay is a great expanse of sand and shingle at low water. It is guarded by a Martello tower and a defensive wall above which was a battery of guns. They were, however, powerless against the naval press gang which landed in the late 1700s and carried off three young men. On the hillside opposite is a conical look-out known as the Pepper Pot.

At the next junction, turn left up a narrower path (if going down to the bay, turn right). The path climbs steeply to a road on a bend. Keep right, passing through an S-bend to take the left turning opposite Varclin Cottage. Turn left again at the next junction. Coming to the main Jerbourg Road, (Route de Jerbourg) turn left and, in 140 yards, right at a crossroad.

This road descends ever more steeply towards Moulin Huet passing a right and a left turning. Bear left uphill on a narrow road and watch for railings on the right, which mark the head of a few steps descending to the cliff path. The cliff path goes back to the starting point, with an occasional sign stone marked 'Jerbourg' or 'Cliff Path' for guidance. The detached rocks at the end of the headland are called the Pea Stacks and various legends attach to the third peak from the end, which looks something like a cowled monk. He was known as Le Petit Bonhomme Andriou and fishermen would salute him as they passed. The Doyle column which soon appears ahead is a memorial to General Sir John Doyle. The original memorial was demolished by the Germans, as it made a good landmark. Today's smaller version was built in 1953. It stands on part of the old earth wall of Jerbourg Castle, whose natural seaward defences can be seen from here. As you pass the steps above Petit Port, you are treading the tracks of a commando landing party of World War II.

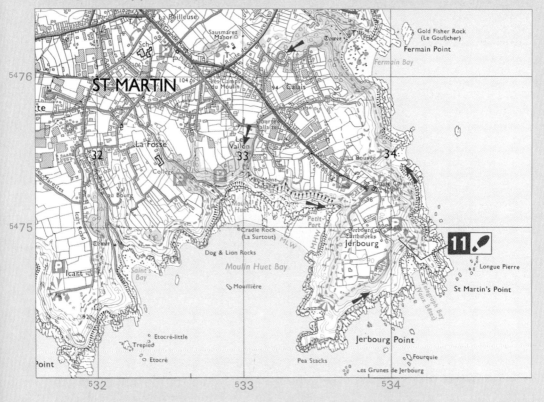

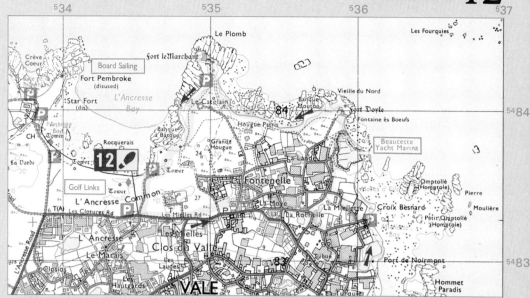

Quarries

Allow 1½ hours **GUERNSEY**

Guernsey is granite country, and this walk takes in granite outcrops, a marina converted from a granite quarry, and a 5000-year-old chambered tomb, made of massive granite slabs. Some of the best granite used in England came from Guernsey, including the steps of St Paul's Cathedral.

Start at the car park by L'Ancresse Lodge Hotel (WV345834). *Walk on the grass beside the main road, with the common on the left and the road on the right. Opposite the bus-turning loop on the far side of the road, bear left over the common, making for the white gable-end of an isolated cottage, whose top is seen in a dip between banks of gorse. A path runs that way and crosses a narrow roadway. Go forward past two semi-detached houses, and carry on over another road and into a lane on the other side.* It winds its way through granite outcrops and between walls and gateposts of excellent masonry to meet a wider road on a bend.

Go straight on into the smaller lane, and turn left at the next crossroads. Before turning note the cobbled roadway ahead: it would be prohibitively expensive to make today.

At the next junction keep right through a sharp bend and enjoy the good view of Paradis quarry, now an emergency reservoir and a sanctuary for wildfowl. *Take the next left turning. After the houses, a right bend is reached, with a mound on the right.* This hides the Déhus Dolmen, one of the island's largest passage tombs and some 5000 years old. It can be entered.

Take the next left turning, the Rue des Hougues de Noirmont. As it twists down to the sea you get glimpses of another huge quarry, now used as a fish farm. Yet another quarry, further south, is the island's rubbish tip and is nearly full. *After the lane has taken a final twist away from the sea, turn right on another winding lane (not the track on the corner).* The Chapel of St Magloire, the 6th-century missionary saint, once stood here. With St Sampson, he brought Christianity to Guernsey.

At the staggered crossroads turn right and then right

L'Ancresse is still ringed by defences

at the end into Beaucette Marina. This great quarry was turned into a marina by blasting away the neck of land which separated it from the sea. In 1967 the owner of the quarry arranged for the Royal Marines to do the blasting as a training exercise in exchange for food and accommodation. But the exercise that was planned to take a few days finally took nine months. The quarry walls extend 30ft above sea level, providing one of the most sheltered moorings in Guernsey.

Leave the marina with the sea on the right and walk over the Common to the white watch house. Just beyond it is Fort Doyle, built as part of the British response to the fortification of Cherbourg in the mid-19th century. From the gun platform there are fine views over the northern approaches to Guernsey, including Alderney and Cap de la Hague.

The walk now follows the coastal path round Fontenelle Bay, past a Martello tower to Fort Le Marchant. Fort Le Marchant was built in around 1800. The shooting club still uses the rifle range from time to time.

Return from Fort Le Marchant to carry on around the shore. The route passes a Victorian rifle range and the remains of a German stone crusher which someone with a machine gun used as a target.

Coming to the next Martello tower, follow the roadway from the car park there back to the starting point.

This walk includes Beaucette Marina by kind permission of the proprietors.

WALK 13
Alderney, the Gibraltar of the Channel

Allow 2½ hours

Starting in the pretty town, the walk explores the dramatic and historic coast. The Spanish Armada was first sighted and reported from Alderney in 1588; it bristles with British and German fortifications and there is even a Roman fort. There are planes from Guernsey and the twice-weekly hydrofoil gives day-visitors about four hours on the island in summer, but at least a day should be allowed for a thorough exploration.

Binoculars are recommended for watching the gannets.

From the harbour or airport, go to Victoria Street in St Anne, the island's tiny and charming town (WA573073). Stroll down the cobbled street keeping the church and post office on your left, then turn left at the bottom and immediately right, to the open green of the Butes. Go straight along the road, which soon becomes a path. There is a good view over Braye Harbour, built for the British fleet in 1847-1864. The huge breakwater was once nearly twice its present length. Beyond can be seen Fort Albert and Quesnard lighthouse.

Keep going straight to the coast road, turn left, and walk along the footpath by Crabby Bay. Follow it through the cutting to Saline Bay where there are more forts. Keep by the shore and at the road take the right fork below the towering buildings of Fort Tourgis. As the track bends south, watch for Fort Clonque at the end of its causeway, thrust out into the turbulent waters of the Swinge. Over the water, the Casquets, Ortac and Burhou form a northern boundary to the channel. All these forts were intended to defend a naval base which never materialised.

Bear left where the path branches right for the causeway to Fort Clonque, and climb the zig-zag path to the top of the hill. Follow the path until it ends at a wider cross track, and turn left. The airport control tower can be seen. In 100 yards turn right on to the macadamed road and watch on the left for the semaphore tower which was described as 'old' on a map of 1804.

Follow the road round as it bends left and loses its smooth surface. After a short distance, turn right on to track, leaving the lights of the airport flare path to your right. Keep to the right when the track forks to reach the cliffs above the Garden Rocks, where thousands of gannets breed. Turn left and walk along the cliff top to Telegraph Bay. Opposite the railings, turn inland to get back to the track and return to the road. Turn right into the road, with the airport to the left, and watch for three gateposts on the left, the entrance to the war-time SS concentration camp. A number of concrete posts can be seen, by which the Land Commissioner re-established the land boundaries after the war.

The road eventually bends left by a granite pillar and takes you straight, over the crossroads, into St Anne. The old German water tower ahead is still in use. On arriving at the attractive cobbled Marais Square, notice the story of the Alderney Cow over the door of the pub.

Go straight on past the museum and the 1767 clock tower, and turn left down Victoria Street to the starting point.

Braye Harbour. The still massive breakwater was once nearly twice as long

Alderney sign

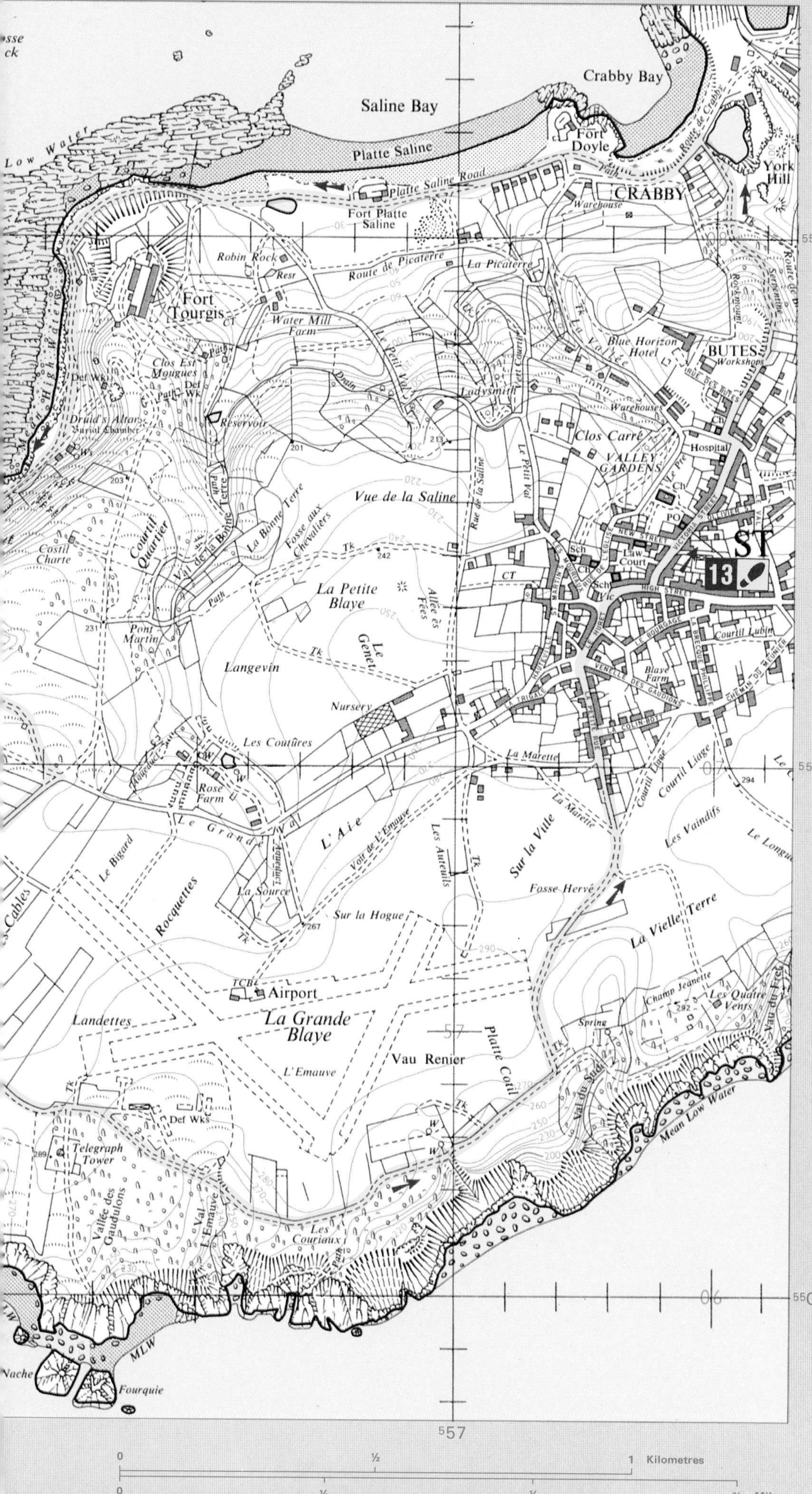

Saline Bay

Crabby Bay

Low Water

Platte Saline

Fort Doyle

York Hill

Platte Saline Road

CRABBY

Fort Platte Saline

Warehouse

Robin Rock   Resr

Route de Picaterre

La Picaterre

Route de Crabby

Fort Tourgis

Water Mill Farm

Blue Horizon Hotel

BUTES
Workshops

Clos Est Mougues
Def Wk

Ladysmith

Warehouses

Druid's Altar
Burial Chamber

Reservoir

Clos Carré

VALLEY GARDENS

Hospital

Costil Charte

Courtil Quartier

Vue de la Saline

Val de la Bonne Terre

Fosse aux Chevaliers

La Petite Blaye

Allée ès Fées

Le Geneu

ST

13

Courtil Lubin

Pont Martin

Langevin

Nursery

Blaye Farm

Les Coutûres

Rose Farm

La Marette

Courtil Liège

Les Vaindifs

Le Longue

L'Aie

Les Aureuls

Sur la Ville

La Marette

Le Bigard

Rocquettes

La Source

Sur la Hogue

Fosse Hervé

La Vielle Terre

Les Cables

TCB   Airport

Landettes

La Grande Blaye

L'Emauve

Vau Renier

Platte Coail

Champ Jeanette

Les Quatre Vents

Spring

Telegraph Tower

Vallée des Gaudulons

Les Courtaux

Mean Low Water

Nache

Fourquie

MLW

SCALE 1:10 560

0 .... ½ .... 1 Kilometres

0 ...... ¼ ...... ½ ...... ¾ Miles

WALK *14*
Feudal Sark

Allow 2 hours

Cars are not allowed in Sark which is slow, peaceful and very beautiful. This walk gives a gentle introduction to its history and scenery. Take the ferry from Guernsey and wear light boots or tough comfortable shoes.

From the harbour (WV477758), tractor-drawn transport can be taken up to the Bel Air Tavern. Walk from there up to the crossroads by the National Westminster Bank and go straight on through the village. The road goes past the island's only post box, to Le Manoir. This beautiful old house was the home of Helier de Carteret, the Elizabethan Seigneur who colonised the island from Jersey in 1564. His arms, a row of four diamonds, can be seen on the top left cornerstone of the façade.

Take the path opposite Le Manoir, signposted Dixcart Hotel, and follow it down the valley past Stocks Hotel. Turn sharp left between the gateposts to pass in front of Dixcart Hotel and carry on up the gentle slope of the narrow road. Just beyond the right bend, cross the stile on the right on to a footpath. This soon gives lovely views over Dixcart Bay to the promontory of the Hogsback beyond. After about half a mile, it joins a road by one of Sark's old coastal defence guns. Turn left to go and see the fantastic land bridge of La Coupée, which joins Great Sark and Little Sark. Before the road was made up by German prisoners of war in 1945, horses would shy at the dangerous crossing and Little Sark had to have its own mill.

Turn back and keep straight along the road for about half a mile. Turn left along the track signposted 'Beau Regard'. Past the Hotel Le Grand Beauregard, turn left on to the road, going round the little dower house. The road swings immediately to the right and then goes straight on to the Pilcher Memorial, a granite obelisk. Here there are magnificent sea views towards Brecqhou, Herm, Jethou and Guernsey.

Go back along the road through a left bend past the hotel and a right bend to pass the ancient duck pond. At the staggered crossroad, go straight on, following the sign marked 'Harbour'. The tower of the old windmill was built in 1571 and is the oldest in the British Isles. The road goes back to Le Manoir, with the Junior School and, just beyond it, the tiny jail.

Bear left at the fork. The road passes the church, the Island Hall, the fire station and the school where Chief Pleas, the island parliament, is held under the presidency of the Seneschal. (The Seigneurie is straight up the road ahead.)

Turn right at the crossroads and right again at the next crossroads into Rue Lucas. The old house called 'La Corderie' was once the island's ropeworks. Rue Lucas is named after Lucas Le Masurier, one of the first Elizabethan settlers.

The road goes past the telephone exchange to the crossroads with the bank at the start of the walk. The harbour is down to the left.

A village scene in Sark

La Grande Grève, below La Coupée

WALK *15* Idyllic Herm

Allow 1½ hours

Channel Islanders and visitors alike hold idyllic Herm in great affection. It is peaceful and beautiful and has its own fascinating history but, above all, it is small. You can explore it in a day and wonder at its miniature government and economy. This walk is easily done in a morning.

The walk starts from the harbour (WV396800). If you land at Rosière Steps, make your way there along the well-marked path. The harbour was built for ships carrying granite, which was exported in great quantities in the 19th century. The Duke of York Steps in London are made of Herm granite.

Walk up to and through the charming little village, turning left on the coastal path, with the sea on the left. The path comes to a tiny cemetery where two bodies from a ship are buried. They are thought to have been cholera victims.

Bear right over the common to the signpost and look for the great slabs of a Neolithic tomb nearby. Notice too the obelisk which replaced a Neolithic standing stone used as a landmark by fishermen. The path goes across the island to Shell Beach, bringing into view the chain of islets known as the Humps to the north and the 300ft cliffs of Sark over the channel of the Big Russel.

The walk now turns right, to the south, with the sea always on the left, along the coastal path. Just after the right bend at Frenchman's Point, the first glimpse is caught of lovely Belvoir Bay.

Turn right up the hill, on the path signposted 'Le Manoir' which climbs steeply to the spine of the island. At the T-junction at the top, make a short detour to the right to look at the Norman chapel and the power station and then return to follow the spine road signposted 'South Coast'. This was built by the monks in the 11th century and the giant boulders were placed by muscle power. Notice the oxen stocks with their little tiled roof, once used for shoeing draught oxen and, further on, the tower of Herm mill on the right.

The road leads on to a stile and a path which soon joins the main cliff path. Turn right. The path crosses Primrose Valley, and comes to the most dramatic part of the path, chipped out of the cliff, and so reaches Point Sauzebourge, overlooking the Percée Strait and the sister island of Jethou. As the path leads north, watch for some fencing on the right which guards the shaft of an old copper mine, a 19th-century venture which failed.

The path descends by steps to the landing place at Rosière Steps and proceeds along the coast back to the harbour. Look for the top of a little conical building on the right. Built in the quarrying days when there were 400 workmen here, it was the island jail, the smallest in the world, with an entry in the *Guinness Book of Records*.

Pastoral Herm

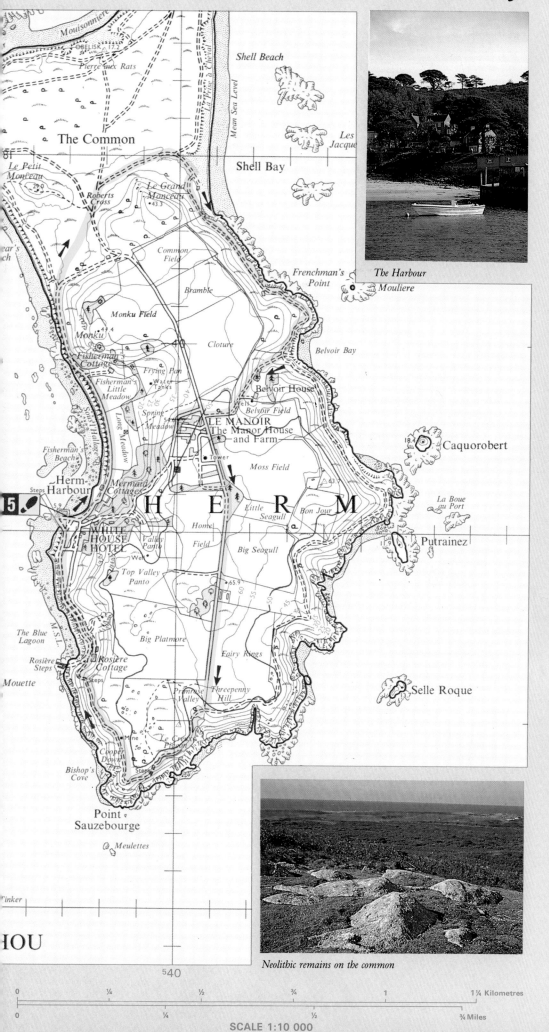

The Harbour

Mouisonnière

OBELISK 17.2

Pierre aux Rats

Shell Beach

The Common

Les Jacques

Shell Bay

Le Petit Monceau

Roberts Cross

Le Grand Monceau 43.3

Common Field

Frenchman's Point

Mouliere

Bramble

Monku Field

Cloture

Belvoir Bay

Monku

Frying Pan

Fisherman's Cottage

Water Tanks

Belvoir House

Fisherman's Little Meadow

Spring

Belvoir Field

Caquorobert

Long Hollow

Meadow

LE MANOIR
The Manor House and Farm

Long Meadow

Tower

Moss Field

18.4

Fisherman's Beach

Herm Harbour

Mermaid Cottages

Little Seagull

Bon Jour

La Boue au Port

5

Steps

Home Field

H E R M

Putrainez

WHITE HOUSE HOTEL

Valley Panto

Big Seagull

The Blue Lagoon

Top Valley Panto

65.9

60

55

50

Rosière Steps

Big Platmore

Fairy Rings

Selle Roque

Mouette

Rosière Cottage

Steps

Primrose Valley

Threepenny Hill

Le Creux Pignon

Steps

Cooper Down

Bishop's Cove

Point Sauzebourge

Meulettes

Tinker

HOU

540

SCALE 1:10 000

| 0 | | ¼ | | ½ | | ¾ | | 1 | | 1¼ Kilometres |

| 0 | | | ¼ | | | ½ | | | ¾ Miles |

Neolithic remains on the common

Index

Page numbers in bold type indicate main entries.

Elizabeth Castle, Jersey

Mount Orgueil Castle, Jersey

How to get to South Coast Ferry and Air Links to the Channel Islands with Ordnance Survey Maps

Routemaster and Routeplanner Maps

The ferry ports of Portsmouth and Weymouth and the airports at
Southampton and Bournemouth are covered by Routemaster map sheets 8 and 9.
These provide route information from
Birmingham, Cambridge, London, Canterbury, Truro and Penzance.
Alternatively use the Ordnance Survey Great Britain Routeplanner Map which covers the
whole country on one map sheet.

Exploring the Islands

For exploring Jersey the Ordnance Survey/States of Jersey Official Leisure Map
is a useful complement to this Guide.

Other titles available in this series are:

Cornwall
Cotswolds
Ireland

Lake District
New Forest
Northumbria
North York Moors

Peak District
Scottish Highlands
Yorkshire Dales

Acknowledgements

The Automobile Association wishes to thank the following photographers, organisations and libraries for their assistance in the compilation of this book. Many of the photographs reproduced are the copyright of the AA Picture Library.

Stuart Abraham 1 fishermen, 3 St Peter Port, 5 farmhouse, 14/15 Castle Cornet, 15 First Tower, 15 Kempt Tower, 15 Fort Ile de Raz, 16 command post, 17 German bunkers, 19 cliffs, 28 Adrian Heyworth, 30 sunset, 31 collecting shells, 32 surfing, 34 St Helier, 35 Elizabeth Castle, 37 radio tower, 37 La Corbière Lighthouse, 38 Grève de Lecq, 40 St Brelade's Church, 40 St Aubin's Harbour, 41 St Ouen's Manor, 41 Fantastic Tropical Gardens, 42 Bonne Nuit Bay, 43 Bouley Bay, 44 Golden Lion Tamarind, 45 La Marquanderie Hill, 46 Mont Orgueil Castle, 47 golfer, 48 Mont Orgueil Castle, 48 Rozel Woods, 48 Rozel, 49 Samarès Manor Gardens, 49 Samarès Manor, 51 Candie Gardens, 51 marina, 52 shop sign, 52 harbour, 54 Town Church, 54 Castle Cornet, 55 Town Church, 55 Weighbridge Clock, 55 Elizabeth College, 56 Martello tower, 58 Oatlands Craft Centre, 59 Vale Castle, 58 Oatlands Craft Centre, 63 Fermain Bay, 65 Fort Grey, 66 Sausmarez Manor, 68 cows, 68/9 Braye Bay, 69 fishing boats, 70 Fort Clonque, 70 Divers Inn, 70 Fort Quesnard, 74 Herm, 74 Neolithic stones, 74 Peter Wood, 92 St Brelade's Bay, 93 La Rocco Tower, 93 St Aubin's, 94 Hermitage, 95 La Rocque, 95 St Catherine's Bay, 95 landing plaque, 99 La Val de La Mare Reservoir, 100 Le Rât Cottage, 102 La Belle Hougue, 105 Fort Grey, 108 Fermain Bay, 110 Braye Harbour, 110 Maria's Pub, 114 Herm, 115 Herm; *M Dryden* 22 Dartford warbler; *Carl Flewitt* 26 Jurat George Baron; *Guernsey Dairies* 62 label; *Guernsey Museum & Art Gallery* 11 notice, 13 coal boats, 29 'Rescue of Johan Collet', 39 Battle of Flowers, 62 cattle, 66 Admiral Sausmarez; *Guernsey Tourist Board* Front Cover Petit Bot Bay, 31 windsurfing, 31 Icart, 67 Moulin Huet Bay, 79 fine catch, 80 riding; *Jersey Tourist Board* 6/7 Mount Orgueil Castle, 32 sailing, 39 Battle of Flowers, 98 La Corbière Lighthouse; *La Société Jersiaise* 8 gold torque, 10 Sir Anthony Poulett, 11 Elizabeth Castle, 13 Weighbridge, 17 Forum Cinema, 29 wreck, 36 Major Pierson, 36 travelling case, 64 kitchen; *F Le Sueur* 21 St Ouen's Pond, 22/3 green lizard; *R Long* 21 marsh harrier; *Stuart McAllister LMPA* 46 ferry; *Maison de Victor Hugo* 52 lookout; *Mary Evans Picture Library* Back Cover St Helier; *Philatelic Bureau* 12 militia stamps; *W F Tipping* 20 butterfly, 20 Laxiflora, 21 hummingbird hawkmoth, 21 poppy, 22 mole cricket, 23 Glanville fritillary; *Peter Trenchard* Front Cover Les Minquiers Reef, Front Cover lobster pots, 8 La Hougue Bie, 15 cannons, 18 Underground Hospital, 24 Senator Reg Jeune, 24 States Chamber, 25 Entrance to States Chamber, 25 Herbert Martel, 27 Belinda Adams, 27 Sark handstamp, 27 post box, 33 Eric Young Orchid Foundation, 35 Elizabeth Castle, 43 Eric Young Orchid Foundation, 44 Jersey Zoo, 44 gorillas, 44 Glass Church, 45 sign, 45 milking, 47 La Hougue Bie, 50 doorway, 50 St Peter Port, 53 Arcade, 53 fish market, 55 choirstall, 55 Norman door, 56/7 L'Ancresse Bay, 59 Beaucette Marina, 58 Vale Church window, 60 Butterfly Farm, 60 Underground Hospital, 61 Little Chapel, 61 llama, 61 signpost, 62 tomato greenhouse, 71 La Coupée, 71 Creux Harbour, 72 dovecote, 72 carriage, 73 cannon display, 73 sign, 76 Battle of Flowers, 77 Heatherbrae Farm, 78 tomatoes, 81 La Coupée, 96 Grandes Rocques, 96 Bordeaux Harbour, 96 Moulin Huet Bay, 97 Beaucette Marina, 101 cattle, 106 Le Trepied, 107 Moulin Huet Bay, 109 L'Ancresse Bay, 113 village, 113 La Grande Grève; *Wyn Voysey* 34 St Helier, 51 Candie Gardens